160
YEARS
160
STORIES

160 YEARS
160 STORIES

Brief biographies of 160 remarkable people
associated with the University of Melbourne

Juliet Flesch and Peter McPhee

MELBOURNE
UNIVERSITY
PRESS

MELBOURNE UNIVERSITY PRESS
An imprint of Melbourne University Publishing Ltd
11–15 Argyle Place South, Carlton, Victoria 3053, Australia
www.mup.com.au

First published 2013
This work is provided by the University of Melbourne under licence from its authors.
Text © Juliet Flesch and Peter McPhee, 2013
Images © various contributors
Design and typography © Melbourne University Publishing Ltd, 2013

Cover designed by Nada Backovic
Text design and typesetting by Megan Ellis
Printed in Australia by McPhersons Printing Group

National Library of Australia Cataloguing-in-Publication entry

Flesch, Juliet, author.

160 years—160 stories: brief biographies of 160 remarkable people associated with the
University of Melbourne/Juliet Flesch and Peter McPhee.

9780522864861 (paperback)
9780522864878 (ebook)

University of Melbourne—Biography.
University of Melbourne—History.
Universities and colleges—Victoria—Melbourne—History.

McPhee, Peter, 1948– author.

378.9451

Contents

Introduction

Juliet Flesch and Peter McPhee

160 Years—160 Stories is published as part of the University's 160th anniversary celebrations. The 160 brief biographical sketches encompass a selection of remarkable individuals associated with the University since its foundation in 1853.

Such an enterprise obviously involves difficult choices. There have been hundreds of thousands of staff and students at the University of Melbourne: all have a story to tell. The best we can hope is that, while many eminently noteworthy people have been omitted, all those included are, for very different reasons, memorable.

Current staff and students of the University, including Professors Emeritus and honorary Fellows, were excluded from our project, as were donors, although their support has been widely acknowledged and is felt daily. Without them, the University as we know it would simply not exist.

The nature of the association which the individuals who were selected had with the University was of various kinds. In many cases their careers and accomplishments lay outside the University, while some of the people included spent most of their lives in the University. One did not live even to finish his undergraduate studies, but he is remembered by his contemporaries as an enduring influence. All enlivened 'the Melbourne experience' for their fellows and affected the lives of many.

Some general intentions guided our choice. We wished to highlight the accomplishment of women of the University, and it is only in recent years that we find significant numbers of them among the Professors. Their absence from the highest academic ranks does not mean that women were insignificant in their academic influence, and we have sought to include a selection of those whose scholarship and dedication to teaching inspired many who achieved greater public recognition and more brilliant careers.

Members of the professional staff are often poorly represented in university histories, so we have sought to pay tribute here to some of the Laboratory Managers, Librarians and others whose work enriched and enabled the scholarly work of others.

We sought to cover all aspects of University life, but equal representation from every Faculty or Division was not our aim. The very history of the University precludes this, since Faculties were not all established at the same time and are not uniform in size. For the same reason, it was not possible to separate candidates into four equal forty-year groups. It soon became obvious that the cataclysms of the two World Wars formed a much more meaningful divide. In the case of some of the 'University families' the working lives of two individuals might span a century of University history.

The University has been fortunate in the volumes of memoirs and histories produced. Among the former, the two volumes of *Memories of Melbourne University* edited by Hume Dow in 1983 and 1985 are unusually rich and readable, and often hilarious. There are brilliant book-length memoirs by Manning Clark, Kathleen Fitzpatrick and Alice Garner, among others. There are very substantial histories of the University by Dick Selleck, John Poynter and Carolyn Rasmussen alongside the many shorter histories of the University, its individual departments and faculties, and the biographies of Brian Fitzpatrick, Percy Grainger, Ernest Scott, 'Pansy' Wright and others.

We know then that for each person included in this volume another three or four of similar attainments, influence and interest might be nominated. We could certainly have written twice as many vignettes as this book contains. As it stands, however, we hope that this collection of brief biographies illuminates the story of the University as a place of diversity, dedication and achievement. This is a sample of those whose contributions have made the University what it is today, an institution which has 'grown in the esteem of future generations', as its motto promises.

Acknowledgements

This work could not have been completed without the helpful suggestions and technical assistance of many people. The first edition in 2005 benefited from the assistance of UniNews, the University Archives and the Development Office. Catherine Herrick of the Historical Unit of the Victorian Education Department provided valuable data on individuals. Suggestions for inclusion in the series were received from all over the University and we thank all who made them. Thanks are due, too, to those people who scoured family collections for suitable photographs, many of them so much more evocative than an official portrait, and who provided further details.

The *160 Years—160 Stories* project was funded through a grant from the University and supported by the Council's 160th Committee.

All errors and omissions are the fault of the authors.

à Beckett Family

Edward Fitzhaley à Beckett (1836–1922) took the field in the second intercolonial cricket match played in Australia in 1852. Not yet sixteen, he took a wicket in each innings. In 1870, he played in the first Intervarsity match and his fine batting was credited with winning the day for Melbourne.

À Beckett's professional life was less distinguished. He was Registrar of the University of Melbourne from 1864 until 1901. Just three months after the celebration of Federation and brilliant ceremony to mark the awarding of an honorary degree to the future King George V, the University was plunged into a financial scandal in which à Beckett was embroiled. He had borrowed large sums of money from Frederick Thomas Dickson, the fraudulent University Accountant, apparently unaware of both the impropriety of borrowing from his staff and of Dickson's depredations.

His kinswoman by marriage, Ada Mary à Beckett (1872–1948), is remembered for better reasons. She was the University's first female lecturer, appointed part-time in 1901 during Baldwin Spencer's Australian anthropological tour. She had occupied various part-time temporary positions in biology since 1898.

Her concurrent secondary teaching career began in 1893. She was employed at Melbourne Church of England Girls' Grammar School as well as several other Melbourne girls' schools and the Working Men's College in Geelong before taking up an appointment as head of the biology department at Scotch College in 1921. She retired in 1937, remembered as a highly competent teacher of students who went on to medical and scientific careers.

Ada à Beckett was foundation vice-president of the Free Kindergarten Union of Victoria. She served as president from 1919 to 1939 and was subsequently named president for life. She was active in the establishment of the Kindergarten Training College at Kew, where she taught physiology and hygiene.

President of the Lyceum Club from 1926 to 1928, à Beckett was also a member of the National Council of Women and the Victoria League, founder of the Australian Association for Pre-School Child Development and the Women Graduates Association, and chair of the Janet Clarke Hall Committee.

Leonhard Adam (1891–1960)

Leonhard Adam, like Franz Stampfl, another man with a long connection to Melbourne University, arrived in Australia in September 1940 under less than ideal conditions. They both came on the *Dunera*, which berthed in Melbourne with a cargo of refugees from Nazism who had been interned and then dispatched to the Antipodes as enemy aliens.

Adam, a graduate of the universities of Greifswald and Berlin (LLD 1916), had a distinguished career behind him. His principal research interests were primitive law and ethnological jurisprudence. He had edited the *Zeitschrift für Vergleichende Rechtswissenschaft* (*Journal of Comparative Jurisprudence*) from 1919 to 1938 and had held positions at the Institute for Foreign Laws and the Ethnographical Museum in Berlin until he was dismissed in 1933 in accordance with the Nazi anti-Semitic laws. In 1938 he fled to England, publishing *Primitive Art* (1940) before being interned and deported.

Following eighteen months in detention in Tatura, and after his case had been taken up by Bernard Malinowski, Margaret Holmes and Lady Masson, Adam was released on parole to the National Museum of Victoria, accommodated in Queen's College and employed, under the supervision of Professor Max Crawford, on research into the Aborigines' use of stone.

He was employed at the University as a Research Scholar 1943–47, Lecturer 1947–56 and, following his retirement on health grounds, as part-time curator of the ethnological collection from 1958 until his death in 1960. Adam lectured on primitive art and law and gave the University's first tuition on the Mandarin language. His battle for the establishment of a Department of Anthropology and a dedicated ethnological museum at the University were both unsuccessful, but the collection which he built up through an extensive network of personal contacts and exchanges forms a valuable part of the resources of the Ian Potter Museum of Art.

He was made a Fellow of the Royal Anthropological Institute of Great Britain and Ireland in 1945.

☙❧

Wilfred Eade Agar (1882–1951)

Wilfred Eade Agar came to the University of Melbourne in 1919, after having participated in the Gallipoli campaign in the Highland Light Infantry. He had served a year as adjutant to the divisional base at Alexandria before being invalided home to England. Before the War, he read Zoology at Cambridge, then combined a post as demonstrator at the University of Glasgow with a Fellowship at King's College. His convalescence between 1916 and 1918 allowed him to write *Cytology*, published in 1920. In 1921 he was elected to the Royal Society.

Agar succeeded Baldwin Spencer as Professor of Zoology, and introduced the disciplines of cytology and genetics to Melbourne students. Despite initial apprehensions, Agar refused overseas posts and noted on his retirement that he had been able to achieve as much in Melbourne as he might have done in Britain. Notable projects concerned marsupial chromosomes and inheritance in cattle. He successfully challenged the Lamarckian finding of William McDougall relating to the inheritance of the effects of training in rats.

The breadth of Agar's scientific interests (which included a longstanding interest in animal psychology) is illustrated in *A Contribution to the Theory of the Living Organism*, published in 1943 with a second edition in 1961, which he rated his most important contribution to biological theory.

Agar was prominent in University administration as Council member, Dean of the Faculty of Science and Chairman of the Professorial Board, which oversaw the appointment of Raymond Priestley as the first full-time Vice-Chancellor. He was President of the Royal Society of Victoria in 1927–28 and on its council for twenty years.

The Agar family lived on Professors Walk in the University grounds until 1948 and Peter MacCallum's daughter Monica recalls that, on the death of their mother, Mrs Agar stood almost *in loco parentis* to the MacCallum children living in a house on Tin Alley.

The Agars' son Wilfred Talbot Agar (1910–2000) graduated in Medicine in 1934. After working as the first Nuffield Dominion Demonstrator in Physiology at Oxford, he volunteered at the outbreak of World War II with the Royal Australian Military Corp and was appointed Officer Commanding a Field Transfusion Unit. On his return to Australia he was appointed Senior Lecturer then Reader in Physiology at Melbourne, where he worked until 1966. In retirement in the Victorian Western District, one of his greatest finds was that some of its underground waters contained toxic levels of magnesium salts.

☙❧

Betty Allan (1905–52)

Frances Elizabeth Allan took her BA, DipEd and MA from the University of Melbourne, sharing the Dixson and Wyselaskie scholarships for mathematics in 1926. She won the Nanson Scholarship for her postgraduate work on solitary waves at the common boundary of two liquids, and in 1928 attended Newnham College, Cambridge, on a two-year studentship from the Council for Scientific and Industrial Research, which permitted her to study statistical methods applied to agriculture.

After a short period at Rothamsted Experimental Station, Harpenden, during which Sir Ronald Fisher commented on her 'rare gift for first-class mathematics', Allan returned in 1930 to the CSIR Division of Plant Industry as its first biometrician.

During her time with CSIR, Allan provided mathematical and statistical assistance to all six divisions and her work may be considered as the nucleus of CSIRO's Division of Mathematics and Statistics. As well as providing statistical work on climatic data, plant diseases and pest control, she lectured in pure mathematics and statistical theory and method at the Canberra University College between 1932 and 1937. She was a foundation member of the Australian Institute of Agricultural Science for which, in 1936, she wrote a set of instructional papers on the application of statistical methods to agriculture, as well as delivering sixteen lectures to CSIR staff.

Obliged by Australian Public Service rules to resign on her marriage in April 1940 to Patrick Joseph Calvert, Allan was given the exceptional option of remaining in her position until the end of the year. She continued to lecture part-time at the Australian Forestry School and undertook research for the Commonwealth Bureau of Census and Statistics.

Motherhood brought new interests and commitments, and Mrs Calvert served as secretary of the Canberra Nursery Kindergarten Society from 1943 to 1944 and president from 1944 to 1946 of the Canberra Mothercraft Society. Her early death of hypertensive cerebral haemorrhage deprived Canberra of one of Australia's best-known mathematicians and a great community worker.

☙

Arthur Barton Pilgrim Amies (1892–1976)

Arthur Amies came from Western Australia to study Dental Science at the University, graduating BDSc in 1924, after which he studied in Edinburgh and spent a year in London, Vienna and the United States before returning to Melbourne and working towards his DDSc, which he took in 1929. In 1933 he gained his diploma of laryngology and otology. He became a fellow of the Royal Australasian College of Surgeons in 1934 and was appointed Professor of Dental Science the same year, an appointment which carried with it those of Dean of the Faculty, Principal of the Australian College of Dentistry and Dean of the Dental Hospital.

Amies was convinced from the outset of the need to establish an independent dental hospital and school, and equally determined that the new facility should offer inpatient accommodation. The hospital was opened in 1963, nearly thirty years after Amies had been appointed. He retired in 1967, in which year the Arthur Amies Ward was named.

He was resolutely opposed to fluoridation of the water supply, an issue on which the population at large as well as dentists were divided.

In World War II Amies served with the 4th Australian General Hospital in Tobruk and in a faciomaxillary and plastic unit attached to the 2nd Australian General Hospital in Egypt. He was nominated to Legacy in 1945 and served as its president ten years later.

Amies served on the Council of Queen's College from 1945 to 1976, chaired the Professorial Board in 1956, and briefly acted as Vice-Chancellor on two occasions. A formal man, he was not averse to the ceremonial aspect of University life; indeed, the *Australian Dictionary of Biography* tells us that he was 'happiest in full academic dress, or in white tie and decorations'.

Shirley Aldythea Andrews (1915–2001)

Shirley Andrews (BSc 1938) led a life of passionate commitment to a very wide range of activities and concerns. During her student years, while she studied Science, she was a founding member both of the Melbourne University Ski Club and of the Council Against War and Fascism. She was also, from the 1930s, a folklorist and dancer, studying with the Borovansky Ballet and Unity Dance Group, and researching Australian traditional dance.

During World War II, Andrews worked in the Veterinary Research Unit, followed by five years at CSIRO. For over twenty years she worked at the Royal Park Psychiatric Hospital as Senior Biochemist, involved with John Cade in the development of lithium treatment of manic depression.

Her interest in dance, for which she was made a Life Member of both the Victorian Folk Music Club and the Folk and Dance Society of Victoria, led to two books: *Take Your Partners: Traditional Dancing in Australia* and *Two Hundred Years of Dancing in Australia*.

It is, however, as a human rights activist that Shirley Andrews is best known. Her commitment to Aboriginal rights dates from 1951, when she joined the Victorian Council for Aboriginal Rights. In 1958 she brought together nine state-based bodies to form the Federal Council for Aboriginal Advancement, later known as the Federal Council for the Advancement of Aborigines and Torres Straits Islanders. FCAATSI played a vital part in organising the national petition for a referendum to give the Commonwealth Government more responsibility in Indigenous affairs and in the successful campaign to have Indigenous Australians counted in the Commonwealth Census.

Her commitment to the rights of Aboriginal Australians did not wane with time. At the age of eighty-five, only months before her death, Shirley Andrews joined the Reconciliation march across the Sydney Harbour Bridge in a wheelchair.

Florence Austral (1894–1968)

Like Nellie Melba, Elsa Stralia and June Bronhill, Florence Austral adopted her professional name as a tribute to her native land. She was born Florence Wilson and until 1921 performed under the name of her Syrian first husband as Florence Fawaz.

Austral entered the University Conservatorium in 1917 and in 1919, having achieved outstanding results in her second year of the Diploma and first year of the Bachelor of Music, left to study Italian opera in New York.

She made her debut in London in 1921. In May 1922 she was called upon to replace Elsa Stralia as Brunnhilde in Die Walküre. Thérèse Radic tells us that, 'Thereafter it was recognized that Austral was an operatic phenomenon, a tireless worker of easy temperament with a voice unequalled in quality and power, particularly suited to the Wagnerian

Florence Austral as 'Brünnhilde'

roles in which she was to excel.' The following year she appeared with Melba in a program of operatic excerpts.

Austral's second husband, whom she married in 1925, was John Amadio (1883–1964), who had played in the Marshall Hall Orchestra in 1903–12 and taught flute at the University Conservatorium of Music from 1909 to 1920. They toured Europe and North America together for fifteen years, returning to considerable acclaim in Australia after tours in the 1930s.

By the time she returned to England, Austral's performance was beginning to be affected by the multiple sclerosis which eventually left her paralysed. During a performance with the Berlin State Opera in 1930, in Die Walküre, she was unable to stand unaided.

After occasional performances for the troops during World War II, Austral returned to Australia to take up a position at the newly established Newcastle Branch of the New South Wales State Conservatorium of Music. She taught there for five years between 1954 and 1959 before ill-health forced her retirement.

Bage Family

Freda Bage at the wheel (date unknown)

When Anna Frederika Bage (1883–1970) became the foundation Principal of Women's College at the University of Queensland in 1914, she had already undertaken research at King's College, London, which led to Fellowship of the Linnaean Society. She had graduated BSc in 1905 and MSc two years later from the University of Melbourne, been a Junior Demonstrator in 1907 and a Senior Demonstrator in 1913. The same year, she had been appointed lecturer in charge of biology at the University of Queensland.

From her earliest days at the College, Freda Bage actively recruited young women from rural areas to attend university, traversing the state to do so. She drove herself, and from 1914, competed in motor rallies, despite accusations that such behaviour was unladylike. Her interest in flora and fauna led her to the presidency of the Field Naturalists' Club in 1915. She was a foundation member of the Barrier Reef Committee.

Bage was a keen sportswoman. She managed the women's hockey team, which went from Melbourne to Adelaide in 1908, the first Australian team to travel interstate. She was President of the Queensland Women's Hockey Association from 1925 to 1931. Her interest in women's organisations encompassed the National Council of Women, Queensland, the Lyceum Club, Brisbane, and the Australian Federation of University Women, of which she was president in 1928–29 and which she several times represented overseas. The Federation endowed a scholarship for women to commemorate her work.

Freda Bage enthusiastically recruited for the Australian forces in both World Wars, despite the death of her only brother at Gallipoli. Edward Frederic Robert Bage (1888–1915) was a Melbourne University graduate in Engineering, who had worked with Mawson on the 1910–13 Antarctic expedition. His mother endowed a scholarship in his memory in 1917.

Freda Bage was not the only member of the family interested in cars. Her sister Ethel (1884–1943) graduated MA from the University of Melbourne and assumed the management of the Kew garage of Jessie Webb's travelling companion after Alice Anderson's sudden death.

❦

William Macmahon Ball (1901–86)

The obituary of Macmahon Ball in *The Age* paints a portrait of a person of exceptional integrity and charisma who resigned on matters of principle from more positions than most people are ever offered.

He graduated in Arts in 1923, immediately being appointed Research Scholar in Psychology. He lectured in Psychology, Logic and Ethics before taking up a Rockefeller Fellowship in Political Science in 1929, studying in Europe and the UK. A Carnegie Travelling Fellowship took him to Europe and the USA in 1938–39: during the Munich crisis he was in Germany.

From 1940 to 1943 Ball was Controller of Short Wave Broadcasts for the Commonwealth Government, assembling and directing a team to monitor and translate foreign-language broadcasts and provide the voice of Australia overseas. From 1945 to 1948 he was employed at the University and in a succession of overseas posts, first as an adviser to the Australian delegation to the San Francisco conference which preceded the establishment of the United Nations, then as the representative of the Australian Government in Indonesia during that country's struggle for independence. In 1946 he was appointed Australian Minister to Japan and the British Commonwealth representative on the Allied Council, with the difficult task of dealing with the demands of both Douglas MacArthur and H.V. Evatt. In 1948 he had the happier experience of leading a goodwill mission to East Asia.

Following a brief period of employment with the *Herald*, Ball was appointed to the Foundation Chair in Political Science at Melbourne University. He remained for almost twenty years, training many of his successors in the Diplomatic Service and becoming a notable commentator on current affairs in print and on radio.

He retired as Professor Emeritus in 1968 and, in the words of his obituary, 'Mac Ball never ceased from thinking, reading and writing, keeping in touch with younger men who had been his pupils.' *W. Macmahon Ball: Politics for the People* by Ai Kobayashi was published in 2013.

James William Barrett (1862–1945)

The conflagration which destroyed Wilson Hall in 1952 also consumed a portrait of this remarkable, if controversial, man. Barrett's father, three of his brothers and one of his sisters were all doctors. Although Barrett's own specialisation lay in ophthalmology, service in the Australian and British armies during World War I saw him take on a much wider role at the 1st Australian General Hospital at Heliopolis, where he served briefly as registrar and oculist, being also honorary secretary of the Australian Red Cross. Recalled to Australia in controversial circumstances, Barrett succeeded in transferring to the British Army until 1919, earning honours from both the British and Egyptian governments in the process.

Returning to Melbourne (and a house in Lansell Road, Toorak, where wallabies grazed in the gardens) Barrett threw himself—after an unsuccessful attempt to enter parliament—into involvement with the University. Before the War he had lectured there; he now became successively Vice-Chancellor (1931), Deputy Chancellor (1934) and Chancellor (1935–39). He retired from active teaching in 1937. Unpopular with the professors (whom he regarded as employees to be governed), he was notoriously successful in getting his way on Council. The stand-off between the academic and lay arms of University governance remained unresolved during the tenure of Raymond Priestley as Vice-Chancellor and was only resolved during that of John Medley after 1938.

Barrett's contribution to the University and the life of the state was, nonetheless, extra-ordinary. President of the British Medical Association in 1935, he was also the first president of the Ophthalmological Society of Australia and Chair of the National Parks Committee, the Town Planning and Playgrounds associations and the Japan Society, among many others. He played a major role in the administration of the University Conservatorium Symphony Orchestra (later merged into the Melbourne Symphony Orchestra).

With his sister Edith, he founded the Bush Nursing Association in 1919. At his death, sixty-seven bush nursing hospitals and fifteen nursing centres in Victoria stood as testimony to this initiative. Edith Helen Barrett (1872–1939) graduated MB in 1901 and MD in 1907. She was a foundation member of the Lyceum Club and indefatigable worker and office-bearer in the Australian Branch of the British Red Cross Association.

❧

Redmond Barry (1813–80)

A career as colourful, apparently contradictory and varied as Redmond Barry's is as difficult to comprehend as it is to summarise. The judge who sentenced to death both Ned Kelly and the convicts accused of murdering the Inspector-General of Penal Establishments, John Grice, not only acquitted the Eureka rebels but also supported the Discharged Prisoners' Aid Society. He was also a lifelong defender of Aborigines, rarely being paid for the cases on which he spent much time and effort.

The list of organisations he founded or helped to found is both long and diverse, including what later became the Athenaeum, the Melbourne Club, the Philharmonic Society, the Royal Society and the Melbourne Hospital.

Barry is, however, best remembered for his immeasurable influence on the cultural life of Victoria through his role as founder of both the University of Melbourne and the Melbourne Public Library, now the State Library of Victoria. Even before the establishment of the latter, Barry had encouraged members of the general public to come to his own house to consult his extensive collection of books and journals. As founder and first Chancellor of the University, Barry presided over an institution which soon commanded world-wide respect. Ernest Scott, describing him as 'suave but masterful', notes his assiduity in attendance at Council meetings and his hospitality to guests. He assumed a hands-on role in the Public Library as well, visiting it almost daily, drafting correspondence and choosing the books.

Barry never married, but maintained the mother of his four children, Mrs Louisa Barrow (died 1889), in a separate establishment from 1846 until his death. The entire family frequently appeared together in public and Louisa Barrow is buried by his side.

Maurice Blackburn (1880–1944)

Maurice Blackburn graduated in Arts (1906) and Law (1909) while working as a teacher and librarian. Admitted to the Bar in 1910, he established Maurice Blackburn & Co. in 1922. He dealt principally in trade union law, but also took cases involving civil liberties. Active in both the Labor Party and Victorian Socialist Party, in 1917 Blackburn lost the Victorian parliamentary seat of Essendon, to which he had been elected three years earlier, because of his opposition to the war. Later, as the member for Fitzroy, he succeeded in carrying the Women's Qualification Act (1926), aimed at removing discrimination against women. He was elected Speaker of the Victorian Parliament in 1933 and moved to the federal seat of Bourke the following year, holding it until 1943.

Although unwavering in opposing conscription for overseas service, Blackburn lost Labor Party support through his advocacy of a citizen army, based on compulsory national service. After the war, he took a leading role in the reformulation of the Labor Party's attitude towards nationalisation. The 'Blackburn interpretation', supporting non-exploitative private ownership of the instruments of production, was adopted in 1921 and restated in 1948. He was frequently at odds with the party over its hesitant attitude towards fascism and was expelled in 1941 because of his support of the Australia-Soviet Friendship League. Blackburn became President of the Australian Council for Civil Liberties in 1940 and brought many issues before parliament. His opposition to the first national security bill passed by the Menzies government cost him further Labor support.

Blackburn lost his seat in the 1943 election, but it was won in 1946 by his widow, the notable feminist and peace activist Doris Amelia Blackburn (1889–1970), who held it from 1946 to 1949.

❦

Geoffrey Norman Blainey (1930–)

When Geoffrey Blainey spoke to final-year school students in the Friends of the Baillieu Library HSC Lectures in the 1970s, the Public Lecture Theatre was packed to capacity and his audience carried copies of his books to be signed, a tribute to what Geoffrey Bolton characterised as Blainey's 'skills in interpreting technological change in admirably lucid narratives that appealed to both specialist and non-specialist audiences'.

Blainey studied History at Melbourne under R.M. Crawford and worked as a freelance historian, pioneering the field of business history with *The Peaks of Lyell* (1954), *Gold and Paper: A History of the National Bank of Australasia* (1958), and *Mines in the Spinifex* (1960). He published *A Centenary History of the University of Melbourne* before accepting a position at the University in the Faculty of Economics and Commerce in 1962. In 1977 he moved to the Ernest Scott Chair of History, a position he occupied until 1988.

Blainey's most popular works belong to this period. *The Tyranny of Distance* (1966), interpreting the motives behind the British settlement of Australia, brought a new phrase to Australian discourse. His interests range from sports and local histories to the broader sweep of *The Causes of War* (1973), covering over two centuries of human conflict, and *The Great See-Saw* (1988), on optimism and pessimism in Western society since 1750.

Blainey has been a significant figure in public debate. His belief, articulated in public lectures and the 1984 *All for Australia*, that increasing and large-scale immigration from Asia endangered Australian social harmony, caused lengthy controversy.

He was Chair of the Australia China Council from 1979 to 1984 and of the Australia Council from 1977 to 1981. As Dean of Arts Blainey was a notable supporter of the University Library. His commitment of Faculty funds to the acquisition of books paved the way for a million-dollar increase in funding. He was appointed foundation Chancellor of the University of Ballarat in 1993.

Geoffrey Blainey has continued to write and broadcast in retirement, delivering the Boyer Lectures, This Land Is All Horizons—Australian Fears and Visions, and publishing *A Shorter History of Australia* in 1994, *Sea of Dangers: Captain Cook and His Rivals* in 2009 and *A Short History of Christianity* in 2011.

☙❧

Walter Moritz Boas (1904–82)

Walter Boas was born and educated in Berlin and, despite his parents' conversion from Judaism to the Lutheran Church, he was fortunate to be already employed in Switzerland when the Nazis came to power.

He had moved to Fribourg in 1932, having earned his doctorate at the Technische Hochschule in Berlin with a fifteen-page thesis, the shortest ever submitted for a higher degree. His work on the plasticity of crystals, originally published in 1935, appeared in English in 1950 and was reissued unchanged in 1968.

Boas was unsuccessful in his first application to join Melbourne University in 1937, but was invited to take up a lectureship funded through a Carnegie Grant the following year. Although only thirty-four, he had already published over two dozen papers. His course on the physics of metals was the first of its kind to be offered in the British Commonwealth.

Because his spoken English was still poor, Boas took great pains with his lecture notes for students, which formed the basis of *An Introduction to the Physics of Metals and Alloys* (1947).

Although Boas and his wife were classified as 'enemy aliens' when war broke out, they were granted 'refugee alien' status in 1943 and became Australian citizens in 1944. They already spoke only English at home and ceremonially burned their German passports shortly after arriving in Australia.

In 1947, frustrated by the lack of research opportunities at the University, Boas became Principal Research Scientist in the CSIR (later CSIRO) Section of Tribophysics. In 1949, although somewhat ambivalent about accepting an administrative position, he became Chief of the Division of Tribophysics, a position he occupied for twenty years. His tenure was remarkable for a steady output of scientific papers, together with close relations with industry, to which the Division provided advice on a range of physical and chemical problems.

He also continued to lecture at the University and returned to the Department of Metallurgy after his retirement from CSIRO, publishing *Properties and Structures of Solids* in 1971. The Walter Boas Building on Wilson Avenue is named in his honour.

ᘓᘔ

Bourke Family

Colin Bourke (1936–) graduated BCom in 1974 and BEd in 1976 after a twenty-year career as a school teacher at primary and secondary level. When he was appointed Principal of Whittlesea Primary School in 1971, he was the first Aborigine to reach such a position. In 1975 he established the Aboriginal Education Branch in the Victorian Department of Education, taking up the position of Director of the Monash University Aboriginal Research Centre from 1977 to 1981.

He was Assistant Secretary of the Department of Aboriginal Affairs 1982–85 and Deputy Principal of the Australian Institute of Aboriginal Studies 1985–87. In 1987 Bourke became the inaugural Dean of the Faculty of Aboriginal and Islander Studies at the University of South Australia, a position he occupied until he returned to Monash as Adjunct Professor in the Centre for Australian Indigenous Studies in 1999.

Colin Bourke's wife, Eleanor Bourke (1943–) was Aboriginal Liaison Officer at the University of Melbourne in 1979, after which she occupied a number of high-ranking positions in the Victorian and Commonwealth Public Service related to indigenous and women's affairs. She was Director of the Aboriginal Research Institute at the University of South Australia 1989–99. As well as degrees in Arts and Education, Eleanor Bourke is a certificated interpreter in Greek.

Colin and Eleanor's son Christopher Bourke (1960–) graduated BDSc from the University of Melbourne in 1982, the University's first Aboriginal dentist graduate. In Canberra he was the Foundation President of the Indigenous Dentists' Association. Appointed to the Legislative Assembly in 2011, replacing the Chief Minister, Jon Stanhope, he was re-elected for the seat of Ginninderra as an Australian Labor Party member.

Colin Bourke has published several books, including *Before the Invasion: Aboriginal Life to 1788* (1980), *Better Practice in School Attendance: Improving the School Attendance of Indigenous Students* (2000) and, with Eleanor Bourke and Bill Edwards, *Aboriginal Australia: An Introductory Reader in Aboriginal Studies* (1994, 1998).

Margaret Mary Bourke (1887–1979)

The financial crash of the 1890s took the Mentone Coffee Palace down with it, and enabled the Sisters of St Brigid to acquire a fully furnished home in 1904 for £2050 to establish a school. In 1933 it was named Kilbreda College. The second principal of the school, who was appointed in 1927 and remained in the position until 1965, was the Irish-born Brigid Bourke, who had taken the name Margaret Mary on entering the Brigidine Novitiate at Albert Park in 1910.

Margaret Mary Bourke was a woman of exceptional culture and independence of mind. Educated at the Ursuline convent in Brussels, she had followed the normal school routine in the mornings, while receiving special tuition in the afternoons in French, Italian, Physics, Astronomy and Botany. Having decided to enter the religious life, she set sail for Australia and enrolled at the Teachers' Training College and the University of Melbourne in 1908. She graduated with First Class Honours.

Bourke believed strongly in the right of women to education and in their leadership potential. Her own scholarship in a specific educational field was honoured in 1971 when she received from the Italian Consul a medal, struck in Rome, acknowledging her pioneering work in Italian language education in Australia.

One of Kilbreda's best known alumnae is Morag Fraser (BA Melb), newspaper columnist and former editor of *Eureka Street* 1991–2003.

Merilyn Bourke (1947–)

Merilyn Bourke's daughter had just started school when Bourke returned to the workforce. She was engaged to fill a part-time position in the Jessie Webb Library in the History Department for six months in 1983 and left, fourteen years later, in 1997. It was her longest period of continuous employment.

In her final year at Melbourne Church of England Girls' Grammar School, Bourke and her partner won several ballroom dancing competitions and an Australian title. Dancing as a career was ruled out when she was seventeen by a major knee injury, however, and she undertook secretarial training. Employment with Qantas allowed her to travel, and fuelled a lifelong interest in British history.

About halfway through her time in the History Department, Merilyn Bourke bravely launched into a very different career, under the name of Julia Byrne. After three medieval novels, Julia Byrne has published three Regency romances. Like many romance novelists, Merilyn Bourke was 'an avid reader, devouring a steady stream of Georgette Heyer, Mary Stewart, Mills & Boon authors and a variety of mysteries'. Surrounded by professional historians, she published *Gentle Conqueror*, the first of several popular historical novels, with Mills & Boon. The book is set in England, two years after the Norman Conquest.

Her novels have been translated into Japanese, French, Greek, Polish, Russian, German, Norwegian and other Scandinavian languages. Her Regency romances in particular are distinguished by their comic touches.

Although Merilyn Bourke/Julia Byrne is the University's only Mills & Boon author, a number of distinguished academics have written popular romance novels for younger readers, among them Sarah Ferber (PhD 1994) and Jenny Pausacker (1948–), whose Dolly Fiction titles appeared under the names of Jane Carlson, Mary Forrest and Jaye Francis. The University has many bestselling authors but, with sales of over 70,000 copies of a single title, Merilyn Bourke is perhaps the one whose work remains the least known by her former colleagues. Her interest is now focussed on family history and such bodies as the Port Phillip Pioneers Group.

❦

Anna Teresa Brennan (1879–1962)

Anna Brennan's three brothers, Thomas, Frank and William, distinguished themselves in the fields of law, politics and journalism. They encouraged her to take up a profession, and having supported each other through their studies, offered the same assistance to her. After an unsuccessful attempt to study medicine, she began her law course in 1906, graduating in 1909. In 1911 she became the first native-born woman admitted to practice in Victoria. She joined her brother's practice: it eventually became known as Frank Brennan & Co, with Anna as senior partner.

She specialised in matrimonial law, advocating the reform of laws which invited collusion or obstructed proceedings and favoured the payment of maintenance to husbands in some circumstances. She sought reforms to permit speedy dissolution of hastily-contracted marriages between Australian women and American servicemen and worked to remove conflict of matrimonial law between Australian states.

Brennan, a devout Catholic, was president from 1918 to 1920 of the Catholic Women's Social Guild, which undertook such activities as hospital visiting, the management of accommodation for women and provision of catechists to lay schools. She had also a special devotion to Joan of Arc and was president of the Victorian chapter in 1938–45 and 1948–62 of the international St Joan's Alliance, a humanitarian organisation with special interest in matters affecting women.

Anna Brennan's mind remained active to the end: she died from pneumonia contracted following a fall from some steps at the University, where she was attending a lecture on nuclear fission.

❧

Ivy Brookes (1883–1970)

The life of Ivy Brookes, eldest daughter of Alfred Deakin, reveals a multiplicity of intertwined careers. Winner of the Ormond Scholarship for singing in 1904, Brookes played in Marshall-Hall's orchestra from 1903 to 1913. She was a lifelong supporter of the Melbourne Symphony Orchestra and a member of the Faculty of Music until 1969. She was a foundation member of the Boards of Studies in both Physical Education and Social Work.

In 1905 she married Herbert Brookes, a man sixteen years her senior, and embraced his political interests. She was involved with him in many conservative political organisations, including the Empire Trade Defence League. Brookes and her husband were prominent in the League of Nations Union and Ivy served on the executive of the National Council of Women and the Playgrounds and Recreation Association, and sat on the board of the Women's Hospital for fifty years.

The family companies of Herbert Brookes were Australian Paper Mills and Brookes & Co. pastoral holdings. He was a brother of the tennis administrator and Davis Cup winner Norman Brookes, whose wife Dame Mabel Brookes amassed notable collections of Australian books and Napoleonic relics and was a tireless charity worker.

In 1915 Ivy Brookes founded the Housewives' Co-operative Association of Victoria, the first of its kind in Australia. In its early years, the Housewives' Association functioned as a consumer co-operative, buying wholesale for redistribution and negotiating discounts for members as well as lobbying on issues connected with women's rights. It eventually supported women candidates and endorsed the inclusion of domestic science in the school curriculum. The Housewives' Association became a national body with about 200,000 members in the 1960s.

Brian Ernest Austin Brown (1933–2013)

The best known group headed by Brian Brown was undoubtedly the Brian Brown Quartet, of which there were four incarnations, but it was only one of the dozen groups led by a musician and teacher who inspired many students of the Victorian College of the Arts.

Brown retired after fifty-five years of combining music teaching with performing: he joined the VCA staff as a lecturer in post-1950 music in 1978, and retired in 1998 as Reader and Head of Improvisation Studies, a course he had established in 1980. Over eighteen years about 600 students attended his weekly workshop class.

Born in Carlton and left fatherless at the age of eight when his father died in a Japanese POW camp, Brian Brown was one of many of notable Melburnians (including Normie Rowe, John Cain senior and Jim Cairns) to attend Northcote High School. Brown left school at fifteen and did not resume academic studies until 1964, when he enrolled full-time in Architecture, while also working full-time playing tenor saxophone, clarinet, flute and piccolo in the Channel Nine Orchestra. He took his BArch from Melbourne University in 1969 and worked as an architect for three years.

Inaugurating the improvisation course was not Brown's only musical innovation. When he met Tasmanian sculptor Garry Greenwood in 1993 he already played the alto and concert flute, pan pipes, synthesisers and soprano saxophone as well as the tenor saxophone. Greenwood built him three leather bowhorns.

Brown married Ros McMillan (1942–) in 1980. McMillan, who took her BMus and PhD from Melbourne University and DipEd and MEd from La Trobe, retired as Head of Music Education at the University in 2004 having joined the staff in 1984. In 1962 McMillan was the first music student elected to the Executive of the Students' Representative Council. She taught at Fintona Girls' School from 1967 to 1969, was Director of Music at Presbyterian Ladies' College from 1974 to 1987 and Director of the Yamaha Music Foundation of Australia and first Australian Yamaha teacher from 1970 to 1974. She is a longstanding member of the Committee of Convocation.

☙❧

Brown Family

'Eddy' Brown (1880–1966) initiated the teaching of Electrical Engineering in the University in 1911 and directed it until his retirement in 1946. He continued to work in the Department long after this date and published his last paper after his eightieth birthday.

He was a much respected instructor, with a memorable turn of phrase. His obituary in *Cranks and Nuts* recalls his description of Schenectady, where he worked at General Electric from 1905 to 1907: 'It is cold there. When you spit it clinks on the pavement', and his annotation of student papers with 'boldly scrawled comments such as "cum grano salis" and "hellbound".' His students nevertheless recalled his concern for their studies and welfare.

His work embraced speed indicators, notably the Squirrel-Cage Tachometer, and the measurement of radio wave-lengths, as well as other electrical measuring instruments, including the Quadrature and Quadraflex Tachometers and Polar Ammeter.

Two of Brown's students chaired the State Electricity Commission of Victoria and several obtained Electrical Engineering Chairs in universities interstate. Having graduated BSc in 1902, MSc in 1911 and DSc in 1926, Brown was awarded the DEng honoris causa during the University's celebrations which marked the Centenary of Engineering Teaching in 1961. One of the University's major teaching awards bears his name.

Eddy Brown gained his doctorate in 1926 and married Dr Vera Scantlebury Brown (1889–1946) the same year. Her career was equally distinguished, although restrictions on employment of married women meant that from that time, she would only be employed part-time. 'Dr Vera' graduated MB BS in 1914 and worked from 1917 to 1919 at the Endell Street Military Hospital in London. As Medical Officer at Melbourne Church of England Girls' Grammar School she inspired regular medical inspections in private schools. By 1925, her lifelong dedication to maternal and infant care was well-established and a report for the Victorian Government with Henrietta Main led to the establishment of the Infant Welfare Division of the Department of Public Health. In 1926 she became its Director, a position she occupied until her death from cancer in 1946. Her advocacy saw a marked increase in government spending and the establishment of the Australian Association of Pre-School Child Development and the Lady Gowrie Child Centres.

George Stephenson Browne (1890–1970)

Like Alice Hoy, G.S. Browne held positions in both the Melbourne Teachers' College and the University for many years. Unlike Hoy, he was to conclude his career entirely in the Faculty of Education.

Browne was born in Melbourne, becoming a junior teacher in the Education Department while studying part-time for his BA and DipEd, which were conferred in 1913. He enlisted in 1916 and was awarded the Military Cross for action in France in 1917. Wounded and invalided home, he was discharged in 1918, returning immediately to England to undertake studies at the universities of Oxford and London. He deferred taking up an appointment at the Melbourne Teachers' College to undertake further overseas study, travelling on scholarships to England, Germany and the USA.

He was especially impressed by the American Project Method, developed from John Dewey's educational philosophy. His major book, *The Case for Curriculum Revision*, published in 1932, had a considerable impact on the training of primary school teachers.

The following year, Browne accepted the position of Professor of Education in the University, which he combined with that of Principal of the Melbourne Teachers College until 1939. His attention turned increasingly towards the training of secondary school teachers. In 1936 Browne initiated the first postgraduate research program in Education in an Australian university. Browne's lectures were recalled by his students as models of clarity and splendid illustrations of teaching technique.

George Browne was President of both the Education Reform Association and Victorian Institute of Education Research and a member of the Australian Council for Educational Research. After retirement in 1956 he became known to television viewers through GTV 9's *Professor Browne's Study*, which ran for ten years.

❧

Anthony Colling Brownless (1817–97)

Anthony Brownless had an unpromising start in the medical profession, being obliged to interrupt his studies in England several times because of accidents or illness. It is probable that his decision to emigrate to Australia from England was taken with a view to improving his health, which, in fact, greatly improved when he did.

Arriving in Melbourne in 1852, Brownless was appointed physician to the Melbourne Benevolent Asylum the following year and physician (later consulting physician) to the Melbourne Hospital in 1853. He also built up an extensive private practice.

His appointment to the Council in June 1855 signalled a change in direction for the University: Brownless presented his first proposal for the establishment of a medical school just eighteen months later. Funding and administrative delays meant that it was only in March 1862 that the first lectures began, with the first Professor, George Halford, arriving in December and beginning teaching in March 1863. Brownless insisted that the course should be a five-year one, making Melbourne the only University except Dublin to offer such a course.

Brownless was appointed Vice-Chancellor (at that time the Chancellor's deputy) in 1858, controlling all committees, and especially the Medical School, for the next twenty-nine years. He succeeded in being appointed Chancellor on his fourth attempt in 1887 and held the position until his death. The historian of the Medical School, K.F. Russell comments that 'His inflexibility of mind and dogged perseverance were all too obvious to his contemporaries, although obscured at first sight by an air of venerable benevolence.' As well as his university posts, Brownless held appointments on the commission on the Yarra Bend Lunatic Asylum, the commission on industrial and reformatory schools and the commission for the Melbourne Centennial International Exhibition. Brownless was a devout convert to the Catholic Church and served for over thirty years on the Catholic Education Committee. He was awarded the knighthood of the Order of St Gregory the Great in 1870 and of the Order of Pius in 1883.

Brownless was also a notable cricketer and maintained his own pack of foxhounds for many years.

Lucy Meredith Bryce (1897–1968)

The occasional panics over the safety of supplies in the Blood Banks of Australia may serve to remind us how much we owe to the work of the haematologist Lucy Bryce.

Graduating in Medicine from Melbourne University in 1922, Bryce held research posts at the Walter and Eliza Hall Institute of Medical Research from 1922 to 1928, enriched by a year in London at the Lister Institute. Following a period as a bacteriologist and clinical pathologist at the Royal Melbourne Hospital, Bryce entered private practice while continuing part-time research at the Hall Institute and Commonwealth Serum Laboratories.

Lucy Bryce is, however, best remembered as the honorary director of the Victorian Blood Transfusion Service, organising a panel of donors who would attend hospitals when donations were required. Her responsibilities included blood grouping, laboratory testing and medical care of the donors. She supervised the implementation of new procedures pioneered during the Spanish Civil War of 1936–39. During World War II Bryce was visiting specialist at the 115th Australian General Hospital at Heidelberg, Victoria.

She was the author of numerous scientific articles and a history of the Blood Bank up to 1959, published under the title of *An Abiding Gladness*. At the time of her death, Bryce was working on a book about her travels in south-east Europe in the 1920s. Her entry in the *Australian Dictionary of Biography* notes that her 'soft voice and manner of a cultured gentlewoman concealed a surprising firmness of purpose. She made large demands on those who worked for her but had the capacity to inspire great loyalty from them'. William Dargie's portrait of her hangs in the Lucy Bryce Hall at the Central Blood Bank.

Vincent Buckley (1927–88)

Seven of Vincent Buckley's great-grandparents were Irish, and Ireland was a strong and constant presence in the work of this Australian poet, teacher and critic.

Buckley took his BA and MA from the University of Melbourne, following this with a period of study at Cambridge. He was appointed Lockie Fellow in the Department of English at Melbourne in 1958, then awarded a personal Chair in 1967. During the late 1950s and early 1960s the Department housed a remarkable number of influential poets, including Philip Martin, Evan Jones and the young Chris Wallace-Crabbe, as well as Buckley. His period as poetry editor of the *Bulletin* from 1961 to 1963 saw the publication of many new poets.

His seven volumes of poetry range from the intensely personal and intimate to rumination on the past and present of Ireland and Irish politics. His critical writing includes volumes on poetry, the novelist Henry Handel Richardson and the Campion paintings by Leonard French.

Buckley was a key figure in Catholic intellectual debate of the period, a time in which the Australian Labor movement was grappling with the Cold War and the emergence of the DLP. He and Frank Knopfelmacher, both on campus and through the pages of *Quadrant*, were influential polemicists. His autobiography, *Cutting Green Hay: Friendships, Movements and Cultural Conflicts in Australia's Great Decades*, published in 1983, provides a valuable insight into the twenty years following the end of World War II.

He was a charismatic lecturer and few who heard his impersonation of W.B. Yeats's fulmination on the modernist poetry of T.S. Eliot would ever forget it. His essays on Slessor, Fitzgerald, Hope, Wright and McAuley remain influential.

Buckley was awarded the Dublin Prize, the University's award for an outstanding contribution to art, music, literature or science, in 1977, and the Christopher Brennan Award from the Fellowship of Australian Writers in 1982.

Eric Henry Stonely Burhop (1911–80)

Eric Burhop's parents were Salvation Army officers: their beliefs inculcated in their son a lifelong commitment to the socially responsible uses of scientific discoveries.

Taking his MSc from the University of Melbourne in 1933, Burhop was the twenty-sixth winner of an Exhibition of 1851 Science Research Scholarship. (Earlier recipients included J.I.O. Masson and L.H. Martin; nine years later it was awarded to D.E. Caro.) He went to the Cavendish Laboratory, Cambridge, to work on an experimental project with fellow-Australians Mark Oliphant and Harrie Massey. His research on the phenomenon of radiationless emission of electrons made him a leading authority on the Auger effect.

Burhop returned to Australia in 1936, completing under Professor Laby a PhD based on his Cambridge work in nuclear physics, and establishing Australia's first research program in this field. During World War II he worked on optical munitions and at the Radiophysics Laboratory in Sydney, before joining the Manhattan Project for the development of the atomic bomb, once again working with Massey. The remainder of his professional life was spent overseas. After the War he worked principally on the nucleus and sub-nuclear realm, in various collaborative projects between University College, London, the European Centre for Nuclear Research (C.E.R.N.) and American laboratories.

Burhop's activism for the responsible use of nuclear power brought him to the attention of both Australian and British authorities. In 1948 the Australian security service opened a file on him and his failure to gain the Chair of Physics at Adelaide University was attributed to his political views. In 1951 his passport was impounded, and returned by the British authorities only after public outcry. He was a foundation member of the Australian Association of Scientific Workers, founder of the British Society for Social Responsibility in Science, and a significant participant in the negotiations leading to the establishment of the Pugwash Conferences, first held in 1957, bringing together scientists concerned about the use of nuclear energy.

❡

Frank Macfarlane Burnet (1899–1985)

Macfarlane Burnet's interest in the natural world dated from early childhood, when he began a collection of beetles, carefully recording his observations and sketches. He took his MD from Melbourne in 1924 and PhD from London in 1928, having undertaken research at the Lister Institute on a Beit Memorial Fellowship from 1925 to 1927.

In 1931 Burnet, who had been appointed Assistant Director at the Walter and Eliza Hall Institute on his return to Melbourne, and Jean Macnamara discovered that there were at least two strains of the poliomyelitis virus. Later in the 1930s, at the National Institute of Medical Research in London, he learned the technique in which a virus is allowed to reproduce after being injected into the membrane surrounding a chick embryo. The science writer Tim Sherratt comments that, 'While modern labs are crammed with sophisticated apparatus, Burnet's main research tools were the egg and the microscope.'

After concentrating on viral research during the 1930s and 1940s, Burnet turned his attention towards immunology. His insight into 'immunological tolerance' was validated experimentally by the English scientist Peter Medawar. In 1960 they shared the Nobel Prize in Physiology or Medicine for this work.

Burnet's theory of how animals produce so wide a variety of antibodies, the clonal selection theory, constituted what he regarded as his most important work. He believed strongly in supporting local scientific research and it was published first in an Australian journal. In 1951, to demonstrate that the spread of myxomatosis was not responsible for a viral outbreak in Mildura, he injected himself with the myxoma virus.

In retirement Burnet published works of popular science, including *Viruses and Man*, two autobiographical titles and a history of the Walter and Eliza Hall Institute. He was a strong opponent both of fluoridation of the water supply and of the White Australia Policy. Widely acclaimed and the recipient of many awards and distinctions, Macfarlane Burnet is remembered in the research institute which bears his name.

༃

John Norman Button (1932–2008)

As Minister for Industry, Technology and Commerce, John Button is remembered as the author of what is still regarded as the Button Plan for the car industry, but his first concern when the Hawke Government came to power in 1983 was in fact the Australian steel industry, which was facing collapse with the threatened closure of BHP in Australia.

Button came to his ministerial appointment with a long career in labour law and parliamentary performance behind him. After graduating LLB in 1955, he had worked with Maurice Blackburn from 1955 to 1974, with a brief period as Research Officer with the British Trades Union Congress in 1959, taking his BA in 1962, and had been a Senator for Victoria from 1974. He was Leader of the Opposition in the Senate from 1980 to 1983 and Leader of the Senate from 1983 to 1993. It was his letter to Bill Hayden which is credited with causing the Leader of the Opposition to step down in favour of Bob Hawke for the coming contest against Malcolm Fraser. This was not the first time he had moved definitively for change: Button had been a notable member of the Participants, a group dedicated to securing Federal intervention in the dysfunctional Victorian Branch of the Australian Labor Party of the 1960s.

As well as his commitment to an industry policy that found a middle path between protectionism and surrender to market forces, Button formulated plans for the steel, car and textiles, clothing and footwear industries, and oversaw tax concessions for research and development, which especially benefited the shipbuilding, pharmaceutical and information technology industries.

On leaving parliament in 1993, as well as chairing numerous boards, ranging from the Japan Australia Venture Capital Fund to the Geelong Cats Sports Foundation, Button became a prolific author, notably of autobiographical works, and won the Alfred Deakin Prize for his 2002 essay *Beyond Belief: What Future for Labor?*

John Button's son James Button (1961–), who took his BA (Hons) from Melbourne, has won two Walkley Awards for feature writing during his many years as a journalist in Australia and Europe. His *Speechless: A Year in My Father's Business* was published in 2012.

John Frederick Joseph Cade (1912–80)

Five years after John Cade's death, the American National Institute of Mental Health estimated that his discovery of the efficacy of the use of lithium in the treatment of manic depression had saved the world no less than $US 17.5 billion in the cost of medical care. He was himself so modest about it that his book, *Mending the Mind*, discusses the use of lithium without mentioning his role in it.

The pioneering laboratory experiments which led to the use of lithium rather than electro-convulsive therapy (shock treatment) and lengthy hospitalisation were undertaken in a disused kitchen at the Repatriation Mental Hospital, Bundoora, where Cade was appointed Medical Superintendent and Psychiatrist after he was demobilised. He had been a prisoner-of-war of the Japanese in Changi, Singapore, from 1942 to 1945. Before the War, following graduation from the University of Melbourne in 1934, he had worked at St Vincent's Hospital, the Royal Children's Hospital and Mont Park Mental Hospital.

In the 1950s, a study trip to Britain led Cade to institute considerable changes in the treatment of patients at the Royal Park Psychiatric Hospital, introducing group therapy and a less authoritarian regime as well as modern facilities. He supported early admission of patients to assist in detection of alcohol-related disorders and supported the use of large doses of thiamin in their treatment.

Although his findings on lithium were published in 1949 and it was widely prescribed from the 1960s, Cade's discovery was not internationally acclaimed until 1970, when he received the psychiatric award of the Taylor Manor Hospital, Maryland, and was made a Distinguished Fellow of the American Psychiatric Association. Many other awards followed.

Cade was a foundation Fellow of the Royal Australian and New Zealand College of Psychiatrists, State President from 1963 to 1980 and National President in 1969–70. He was a member of the Medical Board of Victoria from 1970 until 1980.

James Ford Cairns (1914–2003)

Students passing through Union House at lunch time during the 1990s may not have recognised the elderly man occasionally offering books for sale as a formerly famous minister in the Whitlam Labor government 1972–75. He had also been the leader of the Moratorium movement of protest against Australian involvement in the Vietnam War.

Jim Cairns was born in Carlton. He served in the Victoria Police Force from 1935 to 1944 and the AIF from 1945 to 1946. He completed his MCom and PhD at the University of Melbourne, winning a Nuffield Scholarship to Oxford University in 1950. On his return, he joined the Economic History Department of the Faculty of Economics and Commerce, rising to Senior Lecturer before winning the Federal seat of Yarra for the Australian Labor Party in 1955. Cairns retained a seat in the House of Representatives until 1977, serving as member for Lalor from 1969 to 1977.

He was a charismatic and passionate opponent of the Vietnam War, leading a quarter of a million people through city streets in 1970. Following the Labor victory in 1972, Cairns became Minister for Secondary Industry and Overseas Trade, before being appointed Deputy Prime Minister and Treasurer in 1974. He held these posts until 1975, when he was found to have misled parliament over a letter giving a local businessman powers to seek overseas loans. He retired in 1977.

In retirement Jim Cairns became a familiar figure at markets in the eastern suburbs, where he sold his books on personal development and alternative lifestyle, including *Growth to Freedom* (1979), *The Untried Road* (1990) and *Towards a New Society* (1994). *Jim Cairns, M.H.R.* by Irene Dowse was published in 1971; Paul Ormonde's 1981 biography is *A Foolish Passionate Man*. *Keeper of the Faith: A Biography of Jim Cairns* by Paul Strangio was published in 2002.

☙❧

Carmen Thérèse Callil (1938–)

Carmen Callil's father, who died when she was nine years old, was of Irish-Lebanese extraction, and a barrister and Lecturer in French at Melbourne University.

Callil travelled to England after she graduated in Arts from Melbourne. Inspired by her cousin, 'convinced that I could do anything', she placed an advertisement in the *Times* in 1960 announcing 'Australian BA, typing: Wants job in publishing', and worked for a succession of publishing houses.

The 1970s were revolutionary years in the history of feminist publishing, with Australian women well to the fore. In Melbourne, McPhee Gribble and the associated imprint Sisters produced many titles by Australian authors. In London, Germaine Greer took the world by storm with *The Female Eunuch* and, in 1972, Callil established Virago, one of the most influential and recognisable feminist imprints, with its beautifully illustrated green covers.

Virago published new authors and republished many older works with critical introductions, bringing new readers to such writers as Antonia White, Edith Wharton, Angela Carter and E.M. Delafield. When Virago was acquired by Cape, Chatto & The Bodley Head ten years later, Callil was appointed Chatto's Managing and Publishing Director. Virago became independent again in 1987 following a management buy-out. In 1993–94 Callil was briefly publisher at large for Random House.

In 1994 Callil was awarded honorary doctorates by the Universities of Sheffield, York, Oxford, Brookes and The Open University. She chaired the judging panel for the Booker Prize in 1996, the first Australian to be entrusted with this task. She was a Director of Channel 4 Television from 1985–91 and is a Fellow of the Royal Society of the Arts. In 1998, angered by the Conservative government's choices on the national curriculum for English, which she described as 'stacked with bad poets', she co-authored, with Colm Tóibín, *The Modern Library: The 200 Best Novels in English Since 1950*. A major work, *Bad Faith: A Forgotten History of Family and Fatherland*, about Vichy France and Louis Darquier de Pellepoix, Commissioner for Jewish Affairs in Pétain's government, and his Australian and English family, appeared in 2006.

Kate Isabel Campbell (1899–1986)

Kate Campbell knew she wanted a life in science from an early age, and committed herself to medicine only because she believed there were no jobs in science for a woman. She was admitted to Medicine at the University of Melbourne in 1917, when the number of male students was down because of the war, and was part of the brilliant cohort which included Lucy Bryce, Jean Macnamara and Jean Littlejohn.

Campbell's account of 'A Medical Life' in the collection *The Half-Open Door* is initially a saga of sexual discrimination encountered after a robustly feminist childhood. The Alfred and Children's Hospitals would take no female residents because there were no toilets for women. At the Royal Melbourne Hospital, women were not allowed in Casualty because it was deemed unsuitable for them, but assigned to the ward for refractory or mentally ill patients. 'When we went to the Melbourne outpatients for our first clinic, they chose to give us, a very unsophisticated group as we were, the male VD clinic.'

Campbell's interest in pediatrics was sparked by her work with Vera Scantlebury Brown, who established the Victorian Baby Health Centres Association, and she took over from 'Dr Vera' as their Medical Officer. She set up as a general practitioner in 1927 and became a consultant pediatrician ten years later, lecturing at Melbourne University in Neonatal Pediatrics from 1929 to 1965. Always opposed to a schedule-driven childcare regime, Campbell oversaw the liberalisation of hospital visits when the Queen Victoria Hospital became the first to introduce free visiting hours in the children's wards.

It was in 1951 that Campbell's major discovery was reported, demonstrating a link between excessive oxygen supply in humidicribs and retrolental fibroplasia, a disease which causes blindness in premature babies. For this work she was co-recipient in 1964, with Norman Gregg, of the inaugural Encyclopaedia Britannica Award for Medicine.

જી

Michael Boyd Challen (1932–)

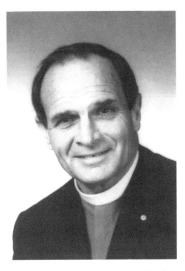

Over the past forty years the Brotherhood of St Laurence, one of Victoria's oldest and most respected welfare organisations, has undergone a fundamental change, although its first concern, enunciated by its founder, Father Gerald Tucker, remains the same. In matters of social justice the Brotherhood is committed to leading rather than following. Its first Research Officer was appointed in 1943.

Michael Challen (BSc 1955) graduated from the University of Melbourne (BSc ThL) and was ordained in the Anglican Church in 1957. From 1959 to 1971, a period of profound change in the inner city, he worked at the Melbourne Diocesan Centre, for the last eight years as its Director. Twenty years in Perth followed, as Director of the Home Mission Department and subsequently as Executive Director of the Anglican Health and Welfare Service. In 1978 he was consecrated a Bishop and acted as Assistant Bishop in the Perth Diocese from 1978 to 1980.

Challen returned to Melbourne in 1991, taking up the position of Executive Director of the Brotherhood of St Laurence at a crucial time in its development, including the transfer of responsibility for some activities to other agencies and the opening of 'retail mega-stores' in Frankston, Dandenong and Croydon. He retired from this position in 1999.

The Brotherhood of St Laurence is dedicated to the abolition of poverty, and aims to achieve this through employment, care of the elderly, supporting communities, early childhood programs and research and advocacy. The titles of some publications of the organisation from 1995 to 2000 make clear the research directions under Challen's leadership: *Issues of Childrearing and Poverty among Asian Immigrants* (1995), *Kooris at Work* (1997), *'You Wonder What's Going to Happen Next': Older People's Access to Services* (1999) and *Poverty in Australia: Measuring Community Attitudes* (2000). In 2008 he published *Sambell: Man of the Word*.

Michael Challen is the most recent Melbourne University alumnus to become Executive Director of the Brotherhood: Geoffrey Sambell, David Scott and Peter Hollingworth preceded him. Since 2001 he has been Adjunct Professor in the Division of Humanities at Curtin University.

❧

William Chamberlin (1900–2003)

While the University of Melbourne was celebrating its sesqui-centenary, it took pleasure in being able to celebrate the life and professional career of an alumnus who lived through two-thirds of its history.

William Chamberlin came comparatively late to the profession which he was to practise with distinction until the age of eighty, and his progress towards it was not easy. After leaving school in 1917 and working for several years in accountancy, he began Veterinary Science studies at Melbourne University in 1924, succeeding despite not having taken the appropriate science subjects at school. His final year was marked by the closure of the Melbourne Veterinary School and Chamberlin was obliged to transfer to Sydney University for tuition before sitting his final examinations in Melbourne.

Chamberlin was awarded the Caroline Kay Scholarship in Veterinary Anatomy and researched the haematology of sheep and cattle. He worked in three states, moving in 1931 to Glenfield, NSW, after gaining his MVetSc. In 1933 he began working as a Veterinary Pathologist with CSIR (the forerunner of CSIRO) in Launceston where he established laboratory test facilities for brucellosis. His accreditation and eradication campaign was so successful that, within three years, eighty-five local herds had been declared free of the disease.

Chamberlin was also instrumental in combating hydatids in Tasmania, using the press and radio to raise awareness of the parasite and the need to avoid infection in farm dogs. He was an active member of the Australian Veterinary Association, serving as Treasurer of the Victorian Branch and Secretary in Tasmania, and re-establishing the Veterinary Association of Tasmania, which had become defunct.

A celebratory luncheon in University House was held in November 2000 to mark Dr Chamberlin's one hundredth birthday. He died on 19 January 2003.

கு

Thomas Cherry (1861–1945)

It is difficult to do justice to the range of activity in Thomas Cherry's professional life. The University's first Professor of Agriculture, whose hands-on experience of farming had come through working in his father's Gisborne joinery firm between matriculation and entering University seven years later, was also a notable bacteriologist, pathologist and cancer researcher.

Cherry's medical degrees were earned between 1889 and 1894. In 1892 he began work at Melbourne University, lecturing and demonstrating in Pathology and Bacteriology. He was in charge of the Department's first postgraduate classes. On his return from a European study tour in 1894, he set up a service for the bacteriological diagnosis of some of the most prevalent scourges of the period, including diphtheria, tuberculosis and typhoid. He regularly examined Melbourne's water supply. Working for the Department of Agriculture, he discovered the link between the fresh-water snail and liver-fluke in sheep.

In 1905 he left the University to become Victorian Director of Agriculture, returning to take up the inaugural Chair in Agriculture in 1911. At the same time, he was active in the endeavour to establish a national laboratory, forerunner of CSIR. In 1916, when government funding of the Chair was terminated, Cherry enlisted in the Australian Army Medical Corps, seeing service in Egypt. As well as working to prevent the introduction of Mediterranean bilharziosis to Australia, he found time to give lectures on history and archaeology for the Army's education program.

The final part of Cherry's professional life concentrated on research into the possible relationship between tuberculosis and cancer, undertaken at the Walter and Eliza Hall Institute of Medical Research and the University's Veterinary Research Institute. It was here that the young 'Pansy' Wright worked for Cherry in 1931 'as wet-nurse to 10,000 bloody mice'.

Cherry's eldest son had been killed in action in France in 1918. Another became the notable mathematician Sir Thomas Macfarland Cherry, F.R.S. (1898–1966), founder of the University Mountaineering Club.

Alan Rowland Chisholm (1888–1981)

When A.R. Chisholm first taught French at the University of Melbourne in the 1920s, all Honours classes were conducted entirely in French. His lectures were beautifully crafted. Lloyd Austin recalled in *Meanjin Quarterly* that 'Chis would first compose a lecture, and then reduce it to half its length'.

A.R. Chisholm was born in Bathurst, NSW, and educated at the University of Sydney and the Sorbonne. After lecturing in Modern Languages at the Sydney Teachers' College, he served in the AIF during World War I and was appointed Lecturer-in-Charge of French at the University of Melbourne in 1921. In 1938 he became Professor of French, a position he occupied until his retirement in 1956. Under his direction the French Department expanded to accommodate Italian as well, and gained international recognition, particularly for work on the *symboliste* writers. Chisholm's own 1934 publication, *Towards Hérodias: A Literary Genealogy*, was recognised as a scholarly milestone.

Chisholm's published output was not limited to scholarly journals or presses, or to French literature alone. His articles appeared in *Farrago*, *Le Courrier Australien*, *Melbourne University Magazine* and the *Argus*. He was a strong supporter of Australian literature, publishing *Christopher Brennan: The Man and his Poetry* in 1946 and *A Study of Christopher Brennan's 'The Forest of the Night'* in 1970, in addition to two editions of the poems of John Shaw Neilson.

Chisholm was a frequent contributor to *Meanjin*, serving on, and for a time chairing, its editorial committee. He was honoured in its 1969 issue as well as by special numbers of the *Australian Journal of French Studies* in 1969 and *AUMLA* in 1959. In addition to his many scholarly books and articles and general journalism, Chisholm published two autobiographical titles: *Men Were My Milestones* in 1958, followed in 1966 by *The Familiar Presence*. They serve, as the *Oxford Companion to Australian Literature* tells us, to document Australian cultural history.

☙❧

Clem and Nina Christesen

By the time Nina Mikhailovna Christesen (1911–2001) arrived in Melbourne with her husband in 1945, she had already accomplished an extraordinary journey. Nina Maximov migrated with her family from St Petersburg to Harbin, Manchuria, at the start of the Russian Revolution, leaving for Queensland when it became obvious that Soviet occupation  was imminent. In Brisbane, she left school at fourteen, working several jobs to continue studying part-time and support her parents.

She taught English, Modern History, French, Algebra and German in a secondary school, as well as Russian at the University of Queensland. In 1939 a casual job tutoring in German introduced her to C.B. Christesen, journalist, broadcaster and actor, whom she married in 1942.

Clement Byrne Christesen (1911–2003), a University of Queensland graduate, founded *Meanjin* in 1940. He was the journal's editor until 1974. In 1945 he accepted the invitation of the University of Melbourne to transfer it to Melbourne and the long association of the Christesens with the University began. Nina Mikhailovna began teaching Russian under the auspices of the French Department, and in 1946 founded Australia's first Department of Russian. The difficulties facing her ranged from a lack of textbooks, qualified staff and even a set of type from which examination papers could be printed, to opposition from colleagues who accused her of Communist sympathies. In 1955 the Christesens were summoned before the Royal Commission on Espionage (Petrov Royal Commission) on the basis of some cultural exchanges.

Despite this, and an occasionally difficult relationship with the University, both Russian scholarship and *Meanjin* flourished under the Christesens. *Meanjin* became a major force in Australian intellectual life, publishing new, influential Australian and European literature and social criticism. Much new Russian writing was published there. Nina Christesen also founded *Melbourne Slavonic Studies*. The Christesens' hospitality was legendary and their house at Eltham, 'Stanhope', was for forty years a meeting place of artists, writers and students.

Charles Manning Hope Clark (1915–91)

Manning Clark is one of a group of twentieth-century historians from Melbourne widely known outside the academy. Generations of Australian History students read R.M. Crawford's *Ourselves and the Pacific* and Keith Hancock's *Australia*, and later generations were brought up on *The Tyranny of Distance* and *The Triumph of the Nomads* by Geoffrey Blainey. The presence of the six volumes of Clark's *A History of Australia* and *Select Documents in Australian History* in school and public libraries ensures that his name is familiar to all who have passed through them.

Clark studied History at the University of Melbourne, going on to Balliol College, Oxford, from 1938 to 1940. After four years teaching at Geelong Grammar School, he returned to the University to teach Politics. In 1946 he was recruited by R.M. Crawford to establish the first course in Australian History, and then in 1949 became the first Professor of History at what was to become the Australian National University. He held this post until 1975.

A History of Australia has been accused of both sloppiness and bias, but its sonorous tones and epic viewpoint found many admirers. Clark examined the European importation of Catholicism, Protestantism, the Enlightenment and their subsequent adaptation in Australia. In 1988 it was turned into a musical, perhaps the most original spectacle of the Bicentennial year. As well as the *History*, Clark edited two volumes of *Select Documents* and wrote three volumes of autobiography as well as many other works.

Manning Clark married Hilma Dymphna Lodewyckx, daughter of Melbourne University's foundation Professor of German, in 1939. They had six children. As well as assisting her husband, Dymphna Clark (1916–2000) was a considerable scholar in her own right. She was an accomplished translator of Dutch, French, German, Latin, Swedish and Russian. She lectured in German at the ANU and, with H.C. Coombs and Judith Wright, was one of the driving forces behind the Aboriginal Treaty Committee in the 1980s. The University of Melbourne awarded her a posthumous LLD in 2000.

One of Manning and Dymphna Clark's grandchildren, Anna Clark (1978– , PhD 2005), published *History Wars* with Stuart Macintyre in 2003, winning the NSW Premier's Prize for Australian History and the Queensland Premier's Prize for Best Literary or Media Work Advancing Public Debate. Her PhD thesis *Teaching the Nation* was published in 2006 and *History's Children: History Wars in the Classroom* in 2008.

❧

Janet Marion Clarke (1851–1909)

Janet Clarke's early life reads a like Bronte novel. Janet Snodgrass, daughter of a failed grazier reduced to living in a modest house in Windsor, was employed at nineteen as governess to the four children of Mary and William Clarke. When Mary died, Janet married her employer and bore him eight children. She also became one of the most influential women in Victoria.

Despite the demands of family and management of 'Rupertswood', the Clarkes' estate at Sunbury, and 'Cliveden', where the Hilton Hotel now stands, Clarke learned French and Italian, presiding over both the Alliance Française and the Dante Alighieri Society. Her support of women's and children's health was manifested in her presidency of the Hospital for Sick Children and the Women's Hospital as well membership of the committees of the Charity Organization Society, the Melbourne District Nursing Society and of the Newsboys' Society. During the 1890s she fed hundreds of people from Richmond and Collingwood from the kitchens at Cliveden. Her Time and Talent sewing circle clothed many.

Her support of female education was most significantly manifested through the Hostel for Women University Students, Trinity College, later named Janet Clarke Hall. Relations between Hostel and College were not always easy, but having provided £5000 for the initial building as well as a further £1000, in 1904 Clarke presided over the University Funds Appeal which raised over £12,000. She was also instrumental in the establishment of the College of Domestic Economy (the 'Emily Mac') and the Melbourne Church of England Girls' Grammar School (Merton Hall), for which she provided the building.

It was after a social cricket match between estate staff and the touring English side of 1881–82 at Rupertswood, that Janet Clarke had one of the stumps burned and placed in a small wooden urn, presenting this first embodiment of The Ashes to Ivo Bligh, the English captain.

&

Ronald Philip Cleary (1926–2000)

Ronald Cleary might have had a career as a teacher of students with special needs had he not seen war service in the South Pacific with the RAAF and studied Medicine at the University of Melbourne under the Commonwealth Scheme for Returned Servicemen.

He had earned a reputation as a fast bowler as well as coming Dux of Mildura Secondary School, and earned a half blue playing cricket at University for six years.

Notable team-mates during this time included Denis and John Cordner, Colin McDonald and George Thoms. McDonald and Thoms opened the batting for Australia in the 1952 Test against the West Indies, becoming the only pair to open together for club, state and country in the same season. McDonald played a further forty-seven tests and became Executive Director of Tennis Australia. Thoms abandoned Test cricket in favour of medicine, becoming known as a gynaecological surgeon and pioneer of laser surgery.

Cleary, once celebrated for bowling two maiden overs to Neil Harvey, and still remembered as one of the country's best fast bowlers of the time, also abandoned cricket in favour of medicine. In 1954 he moved with his wife and two children to the newly established and isolated Soldier Settlement town of Robinvale, setting up practice in a caravan. Valmai Cleary acted as her husband's practice and clinical manager, assisting him as anaesthetist, technician and midwife. She conducted immunisation sessions at the health centre and schools.

Cleary was the only medical practitioner in the district for six years. When Neil Oates joined the practice, the partners delivered four thousand babies and carried out over seventeen thousand operations. The acute shortage of medical personnel in rural areas meant that Cleary continued in practice in Robinvale for over half a century, as well as occasionally acting as dentist and veterinary surgeon.

☙

Albert Ernest Coates (1895–1997)

Albert Coates was born in Ballarat, the eldest of seven children. His formal schooling ended at the age of eleven and at fourteen he left his work as a butcher's apprentice to take up employment with a bookbinder, taking night classes to further his ambition to study medicine. After a stint in the Postmaster-General's Department, aged nineteen, he enlisted in the AIF as a medical orderly. He was among the last Australians to leave the Gallipoli peninsula.

After service in France, Coates returned to Australia and the PMG, working night shifts while he studied medicine, graduating fourth in his class. From 1925 to 1935 he worked at the Melbourne Hospital and from 1925 to 1940 lectured in Anatomy at the University. He rejoined the AIF in 1941 as lieutenant colonel in the Australian Army Medical Corps and was posted to Malaya. Despite opportunities to leave, Coates insisted on remaining with his patients and was captured when the Japanese occupied Padang. Between 1942 and 1945 he worked in the camps in Burma and Thailand, later testifying to the International Military Tribunal for the Far East on the appalling conditions which obtained there. 'Weary' Dunlop later recalled Coates as 'the object of hero-worship and inspiration'.

After the war, Coates worked as honorary surgeon to inpatients at RMH, lectured in Surgery at the University and was instrumental in the establishment of chairs of Medicine and Surgery. He was at various times president of the Melbourne Rotary Club, Council member of the University and a member of the Board of Management of the Fairfield Infectious Diseases Hospital. After retirement from medical practice in 1971, he published *The Albert Coates Story* in 1977.

Although he practised as a general surgeon, Coates was aware of the changes and advances in surgical practice and encouraged both research and specialisation in his juniors. He was awarded an OBE in 1946, and an honorary doctorate of laws in 1962. He was knighted in 1955 and elected a fellow of the Royal College of Surgeons, London, in 1953.

Isabel Clifton Cookson (1893–1973)

Isabel Cookson came to the University of Melbourne from the Methodist Ladies' College where, as well as excelling in several branches of science, she had been a notable tennis player. Later, she represented the University in intervarsity sporting competitions.

Cookson graduated with exhibitions in Botany and Zoology and was appointed as a demonstrator in Botany in 1916. Various research scholarships allowed her to further work on subjects as diverse as the longevity of cut flowers and crown rot in walnut trees. After a period in England in the 1920s, she turned her attention to fossil plants, for which work she received international recognition. From 1930 to 1947 Cookson was a lecturer in Botany and worked on fossil-plant remains. Her research greatly enriched knowledge of the past vegetation of Australia and showed the importance of plant micro-fossils to oil exploration. This work also led to her appointment to head the University's Pollen Research Unit in 1949. In 1952, Cookson was appointed Research Fellow in Botany.

Isabel Cookson's research output of eighty-five papers is all the more remarkable for the fact that thirty were published after her retirement in 1959, when freedom from administrative tasks enabled her to devote more time to research. Although she was a dedicated scholar, the *Australian Dictionary of Biography* tells us that 'in later years she organized her working hours so as to be free to listen to the Australian Broadcasting Commission's Blue Hills and the Argonauts'.

A symposium to honour Cookson's work was held at the University of Queensland in 1971. The proceedings were published by the Geological Society of Australia and she is also commemorated in the award for the best paper in palaeobotany presented at the annual meeting of the Botanical Society of America.

Douglas Berry Copland (1894–1971)

Born in New Zealand, the thirteenth of sixteen children, Copland had a distinguished career in the University of Tasmania before coming to Melbourne in 1924, where he was appointed to the Sidney Myer Chair of Economics. He occupied this position until 1944, when he accepted the Truby Williams Chair.

As well as working to improve the status, employment prospects and recognition of Economics graduates, Copland provided advice to both state and federal governments, chairing a committee which reported to the Australian Loan Council in 1931 on the means of restoring financial stability to Australia. The resulting 'Premiers' Plan' recommended budget cuts and the conversion of internal debt to a lower rate of interest, and is credited with saving the economic structure of Australia. His *Australia in the World Crisis 1929–1933* earned him a DLitt from the University and international renown.

Copland was unsuccessful in his attempt to succeed Raymond Priestley as Vice-Chancellor in 1938 and gradually withdrew from University affairs, accepting appointment as Commonwealth Prices Commissioner in 1939. His policy of establishing price ceilings rather than fixing prices, combined with subsidies to ensure adequate production and distribution of basic articles of consumption at reasonable prices, was admired throughout the Western world.

In 1948, after a brief period as Australian minister to China and attendance at the United Nations General Assembly, Copland became foundation Vice-Chancellor of the Australian National University, combining this with various government positions, notably advising on the Snowy Mountains Hydroelectric Authority. Five years later he was appointed High Commissioner to Canada, during which time he also represented Australia at the United Nations General Assembly. He was a member of the United Nations Social and Economic Council and chaired the Intergovernmental Committee on European Migration in 1953, the same year that he was knighted as KBE. In 1958 he was selected as the founding Principal of the Australian Administrative Staff College at Mount Eliza.

He is commemorated at the University by the Copland Theatre and by undergraduate scholarships in the Faculty of Business and Economics.

☙❧

Coppel Family

Left to right: *Charles, Marjorie and Bill Coppel, Venice, 1955*

Elias Godfrey (Bill) Coppel's (1896–1978) law studies at the University of Melbourne were interrupted by war service. He enlisted in the AIF in 1915 and spent nine months in Egypt before being sent to the Western Front in August 1916. He was discharged in 1919 and admitted to the Victorian Bar in 1922. His publication in 1935 of *The Law Relating to Bills of Sale, Liens on Crops, Liens on Wool, Stock Mortgages and the Assignment or Transfer of Book Debts* earned him his LLD, awarded in 1937.

Coppel appeared several times before the Privy Council and, as well as undertaking a number of company investigations, he was a royal commissioner in inquiries into third party insurance in 1959 and the Queen Victoria Market in 1960. He was Acting Justice of the Supreme Court of Victoria from 1950 to 1952 and of the Supreme Court of Tasmania in 1956 and 1958. Bill Coppel served as Warden of Convocation of the University of Melbourne from 1950 to 1959 and was a member of Council and Faculty of Law from 1959 to 1967.

Marjorie Jean Service (1900–70), a graduate in Arts and Law from the University, and Bill Coppel were married in 1925. Marjorie Coppel was active in the Council for Civil Liberties, notably on behalf of the Jewish detainees from the *Dunera*. She also campaigned for the establishment of day-care centres for working mothers. Her publications include *Food and Health* in 1941, *Our Food* in 1949 and, with Mary Lazarus, *The Making of the Modern World*, in 1960. Marjorie Coppel's service as a member of the Council of Janet Clarke Hall is commemorated in the courtyard which bears her name.

All three of the Coppels' children graduated from the University of Melbourne: Hugh (1927–1951) was a lawyer; Andrew (1930–), a mathematician, is Emeritus Professor at the Australian National University; and Charles (1937– , LLB 1960, PhD Monash 1976) was Associate Professor in the Melbourne History Department until 2002. His research concentrates on the Chinese in Indonesia.

☙❧

Cordner Family

Mrs E.J. Cordner, wife of the University Football Club President, unfurled the flag at the start of the 1907 premiership match between the Brighton and University football clubs, watched by almost 5000 spectators, including the Victorian Premier, Tommy Bent. She had a personal interest in the outcome. Two of her sons were in the University team.

Back row, from left: *Denis, Ted and Donald*
Front row, from left: *Ted senior and Constance*

From that time, the Cordner name has been inseparable from football and Medicine at the University. Henry (Harry) Cordner (1884–1943) took his degree in Medicine in 1909 and captained the 1907 premiership side. His younger brother, Edward Rae Cordner (1887–1963), played in the same match and took his medical degree a year later.

Four sons of Edward Rae Cordner attended the University, also demonstrating spectacular sporting ability. Edward (Ted) Pruen Cordner (1919–96) graduated MMBS in 1942 and MD in 1951. He played for the University Blacks, as did his three brothers, and later played fifty-three games for the Melbourne Football Club. Donald Pruen Cordner (1922–2009) played 166 games for Melbourne, winning the Brownlow Medal in 1946 and captaining the Melbourne premiership side in 1948. He took his Medical degree in 1945. George Denis Cordner (1924–90), captain of Melbourne from 1951 to 1953, played 157 games with the club. He took his MSc with a thesis on the extraction of titanium metal in 1951 and went on to a distinguished career in industry, also becoming Australian Consul-General in New York. The youngest son, John Pruen Cordner (1929–) not only spent a season with the Melbourne Football Club, but also represented Victoria in Sheffield Shield cricket. He took his MSc on investigations on the autoxidation of thiobenzophenone, and the reaction of glycols with lead tetraacetate in 1952. All four brothers played in the (then) VFL as amateurs.

The next generation numbers many distinguished sportsmen and academics. Donald Cordner's son, Stephen Cordner (1952–), with degrees from Melbourne and London Universities, is Director of the Victorian Institute of Forensic Medicine, established the combined Law and Medicine course at Monash University and led a forensic team investigating atrocities in Kosovo. His brother, Christopher Cordner (1949–), captained the University Blacks and was Victorian Rhodes Scholar in 1972. He now lectures in the Melbourne University School of Historical and Philosophical Studies. In 2011 he edited *Philosophy, Ethics and a Common Humanity: Essays in Honour of Raimond Gaita*.

Zelman Cowen (1919–2011)

In a profession which especially values clarity of thought and exposition, the capacity to communicate and convince, Zelman Cowen attained extraordinary eminence. In the words of Robin Sharwood, his students remembered that 'He had the great gift, in a University teacher, of being able to make difficult material interesting and understandable to the average student, whilst at the same time stimulating honours students to investigate matters further for themselves.'

Educated at Scotch College, Cowen graduated in Arts and Law from the University of Melbourne before spending 1941–45 in the Royal Australian Navy. He took up a Rhodes Scholarship to Oriel College, Oxford, in 1947, returning to Melbourne in 1950 as Professor of Public Law. Dean of the Law Faculty from 1951–66, he left to become Vice-Chancellor of the University of New England and then of the University of Queensland.

In 1977 he succeeded Sir John Kerr as Governor-General, and did much to restore community respect for his office. This did not, however, lead him to support its continuance: Cowen was a supporter of an Australian Republic.

Zelman Cowen played a prominent part in public life, writing, broadcasting and conducting adult education classes. He delivered the ABC Boyer Lectures in 1969 and published many professional and general books and articles. He wrote a biography of the first Jewish Governor-General, Isaac Isaacs, and edited the papers of Sir John Latham.

The many honours and degrees with which Zelman Cowen was endowed in Australia were mirrored, if not exceeded, by overseas honours. He was a Visiting Professor at many universities and on the board of countless Trusts. He chaired the British Press Council from 1983 to 1988 and was non-Executive Director of John Fairfax Holdings in 1994–97. The Zelman Cowen National Scholarship for Juris Doctor students from interstate, awarded purely on the basis of academic merit, is the Law School's most prestigious scholarship. His memoirs, *A Public Life*, were published in 2006.

Philippa Cran (1943–)

The first woman to graduate in Engineering from an Australian university took her degree in aeronautical engineering at the University of Melbourne in 1944. Diane Lemaire (1923–2012) went straight on to Farnborough in England, and subsequently to Harvard. By 2011, women were 22 per cent of students enrolled in MEng courses. In 1962 there were just two female students, and they were the first two since 1956.

The arrival of Philippa Cran and Joan Kiang was greeted by the first issue of *Farrago* for the year under the headline 'The Impossible Has Happened'. A measure of apprehension among staff as well as students was evident at this phenomenon, with an officer of the Technical Branch quoted as saying, 'I told Miss Cran that there would be difficulties because the Engineering School is not geared to take in girls.' Nonetheless, he asserted that she represented a 'trend in the right direction'.

Farrago, perhaps predictably, was especially interested in the fact that both young women would wear boiler suits, which the writer identified for those unfamiliar with the term as 'a kind of overall worn by engineering students when doing practical work'.

Philippa Cran came to the University with two first and two second class honours in her Matriculation examination, and when asked how she thought her presence would affect her fellow students, commented firmly that she did not really care and intended to participate fully in her course. She took her degree in Civil Engineering in 1966.

Raymond Maxwell Crawford (1906–91)

Born in Grenfell, NSW, and educated at the universities of Sydney and Oxford, Max Crawford lectured at the University of Sydney from 1935 to 1936 and was appointed to the University of Melbourne in 1937 without a publication to his name.

He had, however, firm ideas on the way History should be taught and immediately set about reshaping the curriculum, in particular embedding in it the subject which he called 'theory and method'. Under a different name, this remains part of the School's offerings to the present day. In 1949 he succeeded in having an additional 'Honours' year, devoted entirely to History, added to the three-year degree.

Crawford embraced what he referred to as the 'synoptic view' of history, a belief that its study must include economic and geographic aspects as well as political and military developments. The discipline of history, he believed, is part of the education of the citizen. His paper, 'The Study of History: A Synoptic View', delivered to the Australian and New Zealand Association for the Advancement of Science in 1939 famously set this out.

Crawford's time in the History Department was briefly interrupted in 1942, when he travelled to Russia as First Secretary to the Australian Legation. He had been there less than a year when ill-health forced his return to Melbourne. In 1946 he appointed Manning Clark to establish this country's first program in Australian History.

Max Crawford's impact on Australian History cannot to be measured in terms of his small publication output, although *Ourselves and the Pacific* was read by many thousands of schoolchildren. It should be measured rather in the numbers of distinguished historians who passed through the Department he transformed and who found the Melbourne School of History so inspiring. They included Weston Bate, Geoffrey Blainey, Inga Clendinnen, Greg Dening, Kathleen Fitzpatrick, Margaret Kiddle, John Poynter, Ray Eriksen, Ken Inglis, John Mulvaney, Alison Patrick, Barry Smith, Hugh Stretton and George Yule. *Max Crawford's School of History: Proceedings of a Symposium Held at the University of Melbourne, 14 December 1998* was published in 2000.

ↄ〜ↄ

Irene Crespin (1896–1980)

Irene Crespin originally hoped to become a musician, but her decision to take geology led her away from both music and a career as a teacher. After graduating BA in 1919, she undertook further geological studies and worked for the Geological Survey of Victoria. In 1927 she became assistant to the Commonwealth Palaeontologist Frederick Chapman, making field trips to East Gippsland as well as conducting research in the National Museum.

In 1936 Crespin succeeded Chapman as Common-wealth Palaeontologist, an appointment which entailed her removal to Canberra. As a female member of the public service, her salary was fixed at around half that paid to her predecessor. From 1946, her position was attached to the Bureau of Mineral Resources. Crespin was an enthusiastic traveller, undertaking investigations in Java and Sumatra, as well in Lakes Entrance, Roma and the Carnarvon Basin.

Irene Crespin was a founding member and President of the Soroptimist Club of Canberra, of which she was made a life member in 1971. She was a tennis player and had a golf handicap of fifteen in 1942. She endowed the Crespin Cup to be contested annually between the 'soft rocks' and 'hard rocks' teams of the Bureau of Mineral Resources and was a firm supporter of the 'soft rocks' side.

Crespin's research output was considerable. She published almost a hundred papers as sole author and over twenty in collaboration with others, a publication record which won her a DSc from the University of Melbourne. Other honours included the Clarke Medal of the Royal Society of New South Wales, honorary fellowship of the Royal Microscopical Society, London, the Commonwealth Professional Officers' Association award of merit and an OBE in 1969. She chaired the Canberra branch of the Territories Division of the Geological Society of Australia in 1955 and was President of the Royal Society of Canberra in 1957. In 1975 she published an autobiographical pamphlet: *Ramblings of a Micropalaeonotologist*.

☙☙

Ernest Cropley (1914–97)

Ernie Cropley joined the staff of the University of Melbourne at eighteen as a junior groundsman under his brother-in-law Charlie Trippit, who was the senior curator. Thus began an association which was to last sixty-five years, interrupted only by service with the AIF in Northern Queensland and New Guinea.

'Croppo' enjoyed a distinguished cricket career with the Protestant Alliance Friendly Society Club in North Melbourne from 1931 to 1947, and the following year succeeded his brother-in-law as senior curator at the University. He held the position until he retired in 1979.

This by no means ended his association with the Melbourne University Cricket Club, however. He had been appointed Vice-President of the Club in 1953 and was, in the words of the Club's obituary tribute, 'at various times committee member, Vice-President, Chairman of selectors, barman, cook and father figure to generations of University cricketers'.

He was equally important to those in other sports. As well as Life Membership of the MUCC (1972), Croppo was awarded Life Member of the Melbourne University Baseball Club and the Melbourne University Football Club. He was Vice-President of the former from 1964 to 1974 and of the latter from 1956 to 1988.

Croppo alleged that 'Colonel', the horse whose work rolling the wicket dated from before 1932 and lasted until 1946, could have done the job on his own, but none of the players doubted that Croppo's own recipe of 'plenty of hard work—early in the piece' was the secret. The other animal of importance in his life was his dog 'Prince'. Three dogs in succession bore this name, watching the matches with their master.

Ernie Cropley was a generous community worker and his attention and affection were extended beyond the youngsters in the University teams. The toddlers at the Alice Paton Kindergarten and the children of members of the North Melbourne Lodge saw him as Santa Claus for many years. He was also a memorable host, who loved cooking.

Ernest Cropley devoted his life to sports at the University and his name lives on in a cup and an Honour Board in the cricket pavilion.

❧

Leo Finn Bernard Cussen (1859–1933)

The law was Leo Cussen's second career. In 1879 he completed his certificate in Civil Engineering and was awarded a full blue, having played for the Melbourne University cricket and football teams. His work as a civil engineer included a feasibility report on a railway line from Alexandra to Mansfield. Later, his experience as an engineer led him to specialise in local government, patent and engineering cases.

Cussen returned to the University at the age of twenty-five and graduated BA in 1884, LLB in 1886 and MA the following year. Initially, he supplemented his earnings by teaching International Law and the Law of Obligations at the University. In all, he was a member of the Faculty of Law for forty-three years. His 1897 article in the *London Law Quarterly Review* is probably the first published there by a Victorian writer. He was a member of the University Council from 1902 and President of the Melbourne Cricket Club from 1907.

In 1906 Cussen was appointed to the Supreme Court of Victoria, an appointment which entailed a considerable financial sacrifice: his salary of £2500 remained unchanged for more than a quarter-century.

Cussen's greatest achievement as a legal academic was in the field of statutory consolidation. His work for the Imperial Acts Applications Act of 1922 involved examining more than 7000 Acts from medieval times onwards, to determine which English and colonial Acts were applicable to Victoria. Cussen's first consolidation of Victorian statutes was presented to parliament in 1915: he completed his second in 1929. Although he was thanked both times by parliament for his great service, the £2500 honorarium proposed in 1929 was deferred and never paid.

Sir Robert Menzies described Cussen as 'one of the great judges of the English-speaking world'. His memory is honoured in the Leo Cussen Chair of Law at Monash University and in the Leo Cussen Institute for Continuing Legal Education.

Dur-e Dara (1945–)

The Australian restaurant industry owes a great deal to women graduates of the University of Melbourne. Notable alumnae in the history of gastronomy include Stephanie Alexander, Marieke Brugman, Mietta and Patricia O'Donnell, and Dur-e Dara. All have succeeded in the overwhelmingly male-dominated world of the restaurateur. As well as Stephanie's, which she ran in partnership with Alexander for over twenty years, Dur-e Dara has been involved in several Melbourne restaurants: the Nudel Bar, Donovan's and subsequently EQ in the Arts Centre.

She is also deeply involved in the Restaurant and Catering Association of Australia, of which she was the first woman President, a position she held from 1995 to 2005. The RCAV was established in 1910 and is the peak industry body. Its Education Division, Hospitality Training Victoria, provides specialised training at the workplace.

Dara was born in Malaysia and completed her secondary education at Presbyterian Ladies' College. She studied Social Work at the University of Melbourne. As well as a career in the food industry, Dara has two other professions, perhaps less well-known to the general public. She is Vice-President of Philanthropy Australia and has convened the Victorian Women's Trust since 1993. The VWT has provided funding to the Centre Against Sexual Assault to develop a code of practice and community education campaign to decrease the level of sexual violence in and around hotels and nightclubs; to the Consumer Law Centre Victoria to address discriminatory selling practices; and to the Key Centre for Women's Health to develop a model of responsive service delivery for young women from Africa and the Middle East. She was awarded the Order of Australia in 1997 for services to the community and to promotion and fundraising activities for women's groups. She is Patron of the Victorian Foundation for Survivors of Torture.

Dur-e Dara's third profession is as a musician. In partnership with David Tolley, Dara is a percussionist and performer of spontaneous composition.

❧

Alan Fraser Davies (1924–87)

'Foo' Davies graduated in Arts from Melbourne University in 1945, joining the staff as a lecturer the following year. He spent periods of study at the London School of Economics Sociology School in 1950 and the Tavistock Institute of Human Relations in 1958. Although his working life was essentially spent in the Melbourne University Department of Political Science, his influence extended far beyond it: he was Visiting Professor at the University of Alberta in 1967 and 1974 and Professor of Australian Studies at Harvard in 1980–81.

Davies was appointed Professor in 1968 and the Melbourne Politics School became the focus of the Melbourne Psychosocial Group. Davies described himself as a 'social psychologist'. He had undergone psychoanalysis himself and saw Political Psychology as having direct relevance for commentators and practitioners alike.

As a teacher, Davies inspired loyalty and emulation. Graham Little, one of his most like-minded and influential colleagues, commented that, although students might at first find him 'odd, elusive and frequently incomprehensible', eventually they 'rose to him, and to their own best work'. For postgraduate students, he was an exceptional supervisor, sending each student away 'inspired with the importance of his or her project and full of new ideas for it'.

Davies was a prolific author, publishing stories, reviews and more than twenty papers of political theory, political sociology and social applications of psychoanalysis. Early works on local government and Australian politics were followed in 1965 by *Australian Society*, which he co-edited with Sol Encel. It marked the beginning of sociology as a discipline in Australia. Among his other works, *Private Politics: A Study of Five Political Outlooks* (1966) and *Skills, Outlooks and Passions: A Psychoanalytic Contribution to the Study of Politics* (1980) greatly influenced his colleagues.

Dream analysis formed the basis of one of the University courses he offered. Davies was working on a book on his dreams when he died and had kept day books and dream diaries for over forty years.

Mary Clementina De Garis (1881–1963)

'Miss Dr de Garis is a woman of medium build, physically well developed, energetical and of serious look. Her every look, her every step, is of great importance and significance. You could see her every morning, going over the Hospital area and inspecting some swamps, which she had formerly ordered to be levelled with earth. A few minutes later, you see her in a hospital circle and so on, until the visit of patients commences.' This letter from a patient in the hospital at Ostrovo, Macedonia, during World War I puts a human, though stern, face on an extraordinary doctor.

'Clemmie' De Garis graduated with high honours in Medicine from Melbourne University. Debarred, by virtue of her sex, from sailing with the Australian Red Cross in 1916, she took herself to England, and served in the Manor War Hospital, Epsom, before going with the Scottish Women's Hospitals to Serbia. She served with such distinction that she was awarded the Order of St Sava, Serbia, III Class.

Her *Clinical Notes and Deductions of a Peripatetic* (1926) sum up part of her subsequent career: 'House Physician, Melbourne Hospital and Women's Hospital, Melbourne; Surgeon to the Muttaburra Hospital, Queensland; Surgeon to the Tibooburra District Hospital, NSW'. After post-graduate study overseas, De Garis took up residence in Geelong, where she spent thirty years as Honorary Obstetrician and Honorary Consulting Obstetrician to the Geelong and District Hospital. During that period, before the availability of either blood transfusions or antibiotics, she delivered over one thousand babies without a single maternal death.

Her brother was Clement (Jack) De Garis, organiser of one of Australia's first national advertising campaigns. In 1919, unable to ship dried fruits overseas, he encouraged domestic consumption with the unforgettable, though medically questionable, couplet:

I fear no more the dreaded 'flu
For Sunraysed fruits will pull me through.

෴

Alfred Deakin (1856–1919)

The early career of Alfred Deakin in many ways parallels that of Theodore Fink, the schoolmate he credited with inspiring him to study Law at the University of Melbourne. Both wrote poetry, became journalists, entered the Victorian Parliament and became ardent advocates of Federation. Deakin was to become the dominant figure of the first decade of the Australian Commonwealth.

His political life did not begin smoothly: he announced his resignation from the Victorian Parliament in 1879 in his maiden speech and it took three contests before he regained the seat in 1880.

For the next decade, Deakin was instrumental in a number of important investigations and pieces of legislation, including the Factories and Shops Act of 1885 and the 1884 Royal Commission on Irrigation and subsequent legislation. Following the defeat of the Gillies government he spent the next ten years as a backbencher, practising as a lawyer, involved with the Theosophical Society and as a delegate to the 1891 National Australasian Convention in Sydney and the 1897–98 Australasian Federal Convention. He played a central role in the 1898–99 referenda campaigns, notably in convincing *The Age* to support Federation.

The first years of federal government saw Deakin as Attorney-General, Leader of the House and Acting Prime Minister during Barton's attendance at the coronation of Edward VII, endorsing protectionism and immigration restriction. He was three times Prime Minister. His second term, from 1905 to 1908, saw the decision on the location of the capital, assumption of control of British New Guinea, the establishment of the Commonwealth Literary Fund and the introduction of the old-age pension. His third term, from 1909 to 1910, was preceded by a bitter battle for leadership of the Liberal-Protectionist party, from which Deakin's prestige did not recover.

He retired in 1913, but chaired the 1914 Royal Commission to investigate wartime food supplies and prices, and toured California in 1915 as President of the Australian Commission for the International Exhibition.

Deakin is regarded as a founding father of the modern Liberal Party. The Federal Division of Deakin, Deakin University, and the Canberra suburb of Deakin are among the places and institutions named after him.

Sophie Charlotte Ducker (1909–2004)

Sophie Ducker maintained a strong and all-encompassing interest in and association with the University of Melbourne for sixty years. Born in Dresden, a member of the prominent Jewish family of von Klemperer, whose banker father was a discriminating collector of antiquarian books, she completed her secondary education in England in 1927 and interrupted her academic studies when she married Dr Johann Friedrich Ducker in 1931. Their son was born in 1933 and they moved to Iran in early 1939. When Soviet forces occupied Tehran in April 1941, the Duckers sought custody from the British who had occupied Southern Iran. On arrival in Australia, they were held from 1941 to 1944 in the Enemy Aliens Detention Centre at Tatura, an extraordinarily hostile environment, as most of the other internees were Nazi sympathisers.

On their release, Sophie began work with Dr Ethel McLennan in the Botany School, and had reached the level of Reader when she retired in 1974. Retirement in Ducker's case was a word rather than a state of being—she continued to contribute to the University by supervising research students, as a member of the Library Committee and as a generous supporter of University causes, including the Friends of the Baillieu Library, for decades. She was a member of the Committee of Convocation until her death.

Ducker was a pioneer in the fields of marine botany, especially algae, and Australian botanical history. She was awarded a DSc in 1978 in recognition of her published work, an LLD in 1993 and the Mueller Medal of ANZAAS in 1996. What a colleague described as her 'indomitable and steely resolve to achieve her goals' was typified in her returning from Madagascar in 1974 with a small number of botanical specimens secreted in her brassiere. Among them were what were later discovered to be two new genera—the *Duckerella* genus of *Delesseria ferlussi* Hariot and the *Ranavalona duckerae* genus of Acrotylacea.

Sophie Ducker was also a prolific author, especially after 'retirement' freed her from the administrative tasks she had undertaken during her active employment. As well as articles in scholarly journals, she contributed to the *Australian Dictionary of Biography*. Her most enduring historical interest was the life and work of William Harvey (1811–66) an Irish botanist specialising in algae. In 1988 she published *The Contented Botanist*, a transcription and elucidation of the letters Harvey wrote during a voyage to Australia and the Pacific between 1853 and 1856.

Diana Joan Dyason (1919–89)

'Ding' Dyason seems to qualify as a 'University child', although she did not live on campus. Her father, Edward Clarence Evelyn Dyason (1886–1949), a successful mining engineer and stockbroker who graduated from the University (BSc 1908, BME 1909), was a collaborator and friend of Giblin, Copland and other academics outside the field of Economics. She recalled that 'at a very tender age I was taught poker by two professors (Ernest Skeats and Samuel Wadham) and a vice-chancellor (Raymond Priestley)'. Ernest Scott, Professor of History, was a favourite uncle.

Dyason's parents believed in equal opportunity for their children and granted them remarkable autonomy and independence. She herself asserted that the recalcitrance of her first pony 'developed any natural stubbornness a hundredfold'.

Dyason graduated BSc in 1942 and MSc in 1945. After working as Research Assistant to R.D. 'Pansy' Wright and Senior Demonstrator in Physiology, she moved in 1949 to a newly-established Department in the Arts Faculty, which later became History and Philosophy of Science. After visiting universities with similar programs in the USA and UK, Dyason returned to HPS, rising to become Reader and Head of Department, a position she occupied until 1974. In 1975 the first Professor was appointed; until then HPS, not represented on the Professorial Board, depended heavily on the consistent and forceful advocacy of Professor Wright.

Independent means permitted Dyason to build on the already extensive collection of her parents and her extraordinarily rich private library was always at the service of students and colleagues. She was generous with both time and money and fought strenuously for University and external organisations, including University (Women's) College and the Australian Conservation Foundation. She was Foundation President of the Australian Association for the History and Philosophy of Science and Australian delegate to two general assemblies of the International Union of History and Philosophy of Science.

Dyason was also a talented poet and water-colourist. In 1984 she was awarded an honorary LLD from Deakin University.

❧

Gareth John Evans (1944–)

John Halfpenny, Foreign Minister Gareth Evans, Nelson Mandela and Robyn Archer during Nelson Mandela's visit to Melbourne, 25 October 1990

When Gareth Evans retired from the Presidency of the Melbourne University SRC in mid-1966, *Farrago* published two appraisals of his term in office. In the eyes of one writer he demonstrated 'increasing demagoguery, intolerance and disregard for democratic procedures'. Another believed he was 'the most dynamic SRC president since the war'. Certainly his tenure had been marked by a high degree of student activism and political commitment, reflecting his Orientation Week exhortation to 'Work hard, play hard, drink hard and think hard'.

Evans came to the University from Melbourne High School, graduating in Arts and Law in 1966–67 before taking his MA in Politics, Philosophy and Economics from Oxford. From 1971 to 1976 he lectured in constitutional and civil liberties law at the University and practised as a barrister, specialising in industrial law. He entered parliament in 1978, serving in the Senate until 1996, and from 1996 to 1999 in the House of Representatives. He was successively Attorney-General (1983–84), Minister for Resources and Energy (1984–87), Minister for Transport and Communication (1987–88) and Foreign Minister (1988–96).

His authorisation of RAAF surveillance of Tasmanian preparations for the damming of the Franklin River earned him some opprobrium and the sobriquet 'Biggles', but it is as Foreign Minister that Evans is best remembered. His involvement in the UN peace plan for Cambodia, the achievement of the international Chemical Weapons Convention and the foundation of APEC won him wide international recognition and awards which include being named Australian Humanist of the Year in 1990 and recipient of the ANZAC Peace Prize in 1995.

Since retiring from parliament in 1999, Evans has co-chaired the International Commission on Intervention and State Sovereignty and served as a member of the International Council of the Asia Society, The International Advisory Board of UN Studies at Yale University and the Carnegie Commission on Preventing Deadly Conflict. He was President and CEO of the International Crisis Group 2000–09, awarded an honorary LLD in 2002 and made a Professorial Fellow in 2009. He was appointed Chancellor of the Australian National University in 2010.

☙

Falk Family

Of the three members of the Falk family with a strong connection to the University of Melbourne, the contribution of Barbara Falk (1910–2008) was by far the longest. Barbara Cohen took her BA(Hons) in 1933 and won the Dwight Prize in History and Political Science. While undertaking postgraduate work at the London School

of Economics, Oxford University and Yale, she taught and researched at the Oxford Child Guidance Clinic. In 1936 she married (Werner) David Falk, returning to Australia when he accepted a Readership in Philosophy at the University of Melbourne.

In Melbourne she taught at Melbourne Church of England Girls' Grammar School, headed Mercer House and, in 1960, returned to the University as a Senior Lecturer in Education. There, she established the Centre for the Study of Higher Education, which she led until her 'retirement' in 1975. From then until her death, Barbara Falk could be found almost every day in the History Department where, as Principal Fellow, she wrote several books and proved an unfailing source of support and encouragement to younger staff. Her 'cheese and chat' lunches for tutors were legendary. *No Other Home: An Anglo-Jewish story, 1833–1987* (1988) and *Caught in a Snare: Hitler's Refugee Academics, 1933–1949* (1998) provide some autobiographical insights.

David Falk (1906–91) had taken his PhD in 1932 from Heidelberg with a highly acclaimed thesis *Logische Grundfragen der Wirtschaftswissenschaft*. He was Reader in Philosophy from 1950 to 1958, when he left for Wayne State University, Detroit. *Ought, Reasons, and Morality: The Collected Papers of W.D. Falk* was published in 1986.

'Jim' (James Edward) Falk (1946–), the youngest of the Falks' three children, took his PhD in theoretical physics from Monash. After appointments as Professor of Science and Technology Studies at the University of Wollongong in 1989, then Deputy Vice-Chancellor of Victoria University, Jim established and directed the Australian Centre for Science, Innovation and Society at the University of Melbourne in 2004. His books include *Global Fission: The Battle over Nuclear Power* (1982), *The Greenhouse Challenge: What's To Be Done?* (1989), *The End of Sovereignty?* (1992) and *Worlds in Transition: Evolving Governance across a Stressed Planet* (2009).

ॐ

Charles Fenner (1884–1955)

Charles Fenner left school at the age of thirteen, but he went on to a distinguished career in teaching and educational administration.

In 1912 Fenner taught at the School of Mines in Ballarat. He took his GradDipEd from the Melbourne Teachers' College the same year, his BSc from the University of Melbourne the following year and his DSc in 1917. Fenner was appointed Principal of the Ballarat School of Mines in 1917, a position he left in 1919 to become Superintendent of Technical Education in South Australia. From 1939 to 1946 he was Director of Education and during 1930–45 foundation Lecturer in Geography at the University of Adelaide.

Fenner was an educational innovator, and Thebarton Technical High School introduced students to the Dalton Plan, derived from the theory of Helen Parkhurst at her school in Dalton, Massachusetts. Under the Plan, students followed an established curriculum, but set their own pace in achieving their goals.

Fenner was a prolific author, producing scientific journalism under the pen-name of Tellurian and about two dozen books which covered his considerable range of interests. They include *Thebarton Cottage, the Old Home of Colonel William Light* (1927), *Individual Education: Being an Account of an Experiment in Operation at the Thebarton Technical High School, South Australia* (1930), *South Australia: A Geographical Study, Structural, Regional and Human* (1931) and *Mostly Australian* (1944).

Fenner and his wife, who was also a teacher, had five children. Their second son, Frank (1914–2010), widely regarded as one of Australia's greatest scientists, was foundation Professor of Microbiology at the ANU and Director of the John Curtin School for Medical Research. He was Haley Research Fellow at the University of Melbourne in 1946–48, working with Macfarlane Burnet at the Walter and Eliza Hall Institute. His paper on mouse pox, first published in *The Lancet* in 1948, is still cited. His autobiographical *Nature, Nurture and Chance: The Lives of Frank and Charles Fenner* was published in 2006.

∽

Theodore Fink (1855–1942)

Theodore Fink was born in Guernsey in the Channel Islands. His family subsequently migrated to Geelong and he completed his secondary education in Melbourne.

Alfred Deakin, a schoolmate and lifelong friend, attributed his own choice of a legal career to Fink's example. Like his friend, Fink was an ardent believer in Federation. He joined the firm of Henry J. Farmer while studying part-time at Melbourne University: he was admitted to practice as a solicitor in 1877 and set up in partnership with R. W. Best and P.D. Phillips in 1886.

He had already, in 1879, become the youngest member of the Yorick Club, a society which led to friendship with writers and artists including Conder, Streeton, Marcus Clarke, J.F. Archibald, McCubbin, Phil May and Tom Roberts. He published in the Melbourne *Punch* and was a member of the Victorian Artists' Society.

Fink was severely affected by the collapse of the land boom in the 1890s and only retrieved his position through restructuring his debts, which also left him with a directorship of the Herald and Sportsman Newspapers Co. Ltd (publisher of the Melbourne *Herald*).

Fink represented Jolimont and West Richmond in the Victorian Legislative Assembly from 1894 to 1904. During this time he chaired the Royal Commission on Technical Education, whose recommendations led to the extension of compulsory education and reforms in the employment of teachers. He also chaired the Commission on the University of Melbourne as well as serving on its Council.

As Chairman of the *Herald* group, Fink was responsible for the appointment of Keith Murdoch as Editor, but opposed his becoming a Director. On several occasions Fink was Australian delegate to the Empire Press Conference. During World War I he served on the State War Council. He was Victorian Chair of the Commonwealth Repatriation Scheme and a proponent of the rights of ex-servicemen. *Theodore Fink: A Talent for Ubiquity* by Don Garden was published in 1998.

Kathleen Fitzpatrick (1905–90)

Kathleen Fitzpatrick exerted a powerful influence on several generations of History students, an inspired and inspiring teacher. When appointed Associate Professor in 1948, she was only the third woman in the University to have achieved this rank. Her assessment of her contribution is typically self-effacing: 'I did some research, wrote some books and articles and served on committees, but I chiefly justified my place by making myself useful in lecturing and administration.' The citation for her LLD *honoris causa* in 1983 puts a different complexion on this: her lectures 'were an unfailing compound of lucidity, scholarship, wit and elegance and it would be interesting to calculate the number of now senior academics who were seduced by them into the pursuit of History'.

Teaching took time which might otherwise have resulted in publications, but two books were influential. *Australian Explorers*, published in 1953 by Oxford University Press, introduced the explorers to an Australian and overseas readership. *Solid Bluestone Foundations and Other Memories of a Melbourne Girlhood, 1908–1928*, published in 1983, joined with her chapter in *The Half-Open Door*, provide a beautifully crafted insight into one of Melbourne's best-loved teachers. *Dear Kathleen, Dear Manning: The Correspondence of Manning Clark and Kathleen Fitzpatrick, 1949–1990*, edited by Susan Davies, was published in 1996.

A foundation member of the Australian Humanities Research Council and Foundation Fellow of the Australian Academy of the Humanities, Kathleen Fitzpatrick was the first woman appointed to the Council of the National Library of Australia. She is honoured by an annual lecture which bears her name. With the generosity of spirit for which she was renowned, her bequest to the University Library of funds for books for History bears the name of her father, Henry Arthur Pitt, in gratitude for allowing her the university education of which he had been deprived.

෴

Margot Elizabeth Foster (1958–)

Margot Foster graduated BA LLB from the University of Melbourne in 1981. Her law practice in Melbourne combines her interests in the law and sport, especially women in sport.

Foster won a bronze medal as stroke of the Women's Coxed Four at the Olympic Games in Los Angeles in 1984 (Australia's first Olympic medal in women's rowing) and followed this with the gold medal in the Women's Eights at the 1986 Commonwealth Games.

She has held many appointments on a variety of Australian and New Zealand sporting bodies, including the Australian Olympic Athletes' Commission and the Australian Olympic Education Commission, the 1996 Olympic Games Bid, Rowing Australia, Rowing Victoria, the Boards of the New Zealand Hillary Commission, Gymnastics Australia, the Australian Sports Commission and the University of Melbourne Sports Union.

Foster has also been President of Womensport Australia, a non-government organisation which represents the interest of women and girls in sport and physical activity. One of its principal areas of concern is to increase the number of women in leadership, management and decision-making in the sports industry. It is part of the Mentor as Anything program, which sets up mentoring relationships in order to further this goal. A second area of attention is that of media coverage of women's sport. Foster has also published journal articles, notably on media coverage of sportswomen. A third is organising the International Womensport Festival, which is a celebration of women's participation in sport.

Margot Foster continues to run a legal practice in St Kilda. In 2010 she was inducted as a member of the Rowing Victoria Hall of Fame.

Garner Family

Helen Garner

Helen Garner (1942–) took her Honours degree in Arts from the University of Melbourne in 1965. Employment as a teacher ended in furore when she was dismissed from Fitzroy High School in 1972 for her frankness in discussing sexual matters and her use of what was alleged to be 'gutter language' with her students. In the 1970s Garner published in journals including *The Digger* and *Vashti's Voice* and worked with the Women's Theatre Group.

Her first novel, *Monkey Grip*, appeared in 1977. This story of a young single mother and her heroin-addicted lover in Carlton won the 1978 National Book Council Award and was filmed in 1982. *The Children's Bach*, rated by some critics among the ten best Australian novels of the twentieth century, won the 1986 South Australian Premier's Award and, in the same year, *Postcards from Surfers* took out the NSW Premier's Award.

Garner has successfully written both fiction and non-fiction. Considerable controversy attended the 1995 publication of *The First Stone: Some Questions about Sex and Power*, an examination of allegations of misconduct in a University college. *Joe Cinque's Consolation: A True Story of Death, Grief and the Law* (2004) and *The Spare Room* (2008) also tell true stories through an openly autobiographical lens. Garner's journalism is notable for its range of subjects—from her baby granddaughter's fascination with a beaded bracelet to a post-mortem examination in the morgue—and its minutely observed, passionately conveyed detail. Her screenplays are *The Last Days of Chez Nous* and *Two Friends*.

Her daughter, Alice Garner (1969–), is a historian, musician, community activist and actor. At the age of nine she played the heroine's daughter in *Monkey Grip* and has since appeared in films, including the campus comedy *Love and Other Catastrophes*, and television series, among them *Sea Change* and *The Secret Life of Us*, and on stage with the Melbourne Theatre Company. Her Melbourne PhD was published as *A Shifting Shore: Locals, Outsiders and the Transformation of a French Fishing Town, 1823–2000* (2005). The following year she published her evocative memoir of student life around 1990 in *The Student Chronicles*.

Alice Garner's father Bill Garner (1944–), whose own father and two sons attended Melbourne University, graduated in Philosophy in 1966, and after a short period of research joined the Australian Performing Group in 1972, beginning a long career in theatre and television as a writer and actor. In the 1990s he and his wife Sue Gore set up an independent theatre company, commonplace, co-writing and producing several critically acclaimed plays. Bill Garner returned to academia in 2006, taking his PhD in 2010, entitled *Land of Camps: The Ephemeral Settlement of Australia*.

❦

Gavan Duffy Family

Charles Gavan Duffy (1816–1903) served in the British House of Commons from 1852 to 1855 before migrating to Australia. He was elected to the Victorian Parliament in 1856 and was an early supporter of Federation. He served as Premier in 1871–72. Like him, his sons and grandson were to make an extraordinary contribution to Australian political and legal life.

His elder son, Frank Gavan Duffy (1852–1936), graduated BA from the University of Melbourne in 1872, obtaining his LLB and MA ten years later. Duffy appeared for the Railways Commissioner Richard Speight in a £25,000 libel case against David Syme of

Back row, from left: *Mrs Frank Gavan Duffy, Mrs John Gavan Duffy, Miss Hetty Gavan Duffy, Mr Charles Gavan Duffy and Miss Geraldine Gavan Duffy* Front row, from left: *Frank, John and Miss Susan Gavan Duffy*

The Age and appeared on behalf of the Commonwealth in constitutional cases before the High Court of Australia. Owen Dixon commented that, as advocate, he could make bricks without straw in open court.

His appointment to the High Court in 1913 signalled a change in constitutional interpretation, with Duffy, Charles Powers and George Rich tending to support Higgins and Isaacs against the remaining foundation members, Griffith and Barton. Duffy refused nomination to the Senate and succeeded Isaacs as Chief Justice in 1931.

His younger son, Charles Gavan Duffy (1855–1932), graduated LLB from Melbourne in 1880, but never practised, having already joined the Victorian civil service. After acting as private secretary to his father during his Premiership he transferred to the Legislative Assembly, and after Federation to the Commonwealth Public Service. He served both Senate and House of Representatives, with well-recognised command of parliamentary procedure, and was secretary to the Federal War Committee from 1915 to 1916.

Charles Leonard Gavan Duffy (1882–1961), son of Frank Gavan Duffy, also studied Law at Melbourne. He enlisted in 1915 and served with distinction at Gallipoli and in France. He was gassed in 1917, wounded in 1918 and mentioned in dispatches. In 1933, he succeeded Leo Cussen as Justice of the Supreme Court of Victoria and was President of the Melbourne Club in 1944. Despite increasing physical disability, he sat on the bench until days before his death.

Ian James Gawler (1950–)

Ian Gawler graduated in Veterinary Science and practised in South Australia, Queensland and Victoria between 1972 and 1985. He is, however, best known for his own survival from cancer and his dedication to assisting the survival of others. Gawler contracted cancer of the bone in 1975, which necessitated the amputation of his right leg. Secondary tumors were diagnosed less than a year later and he was not expected to live. He sought treatment in the Philippines and returned to Australia in the belief that a combination of natural therapies and meditation could reactivate his immune system and combat the cancer.

Gawler advocates a holistic approach to cancer treatment, combining medication with lifestyle and dietary change, and a positive attitude. This approach is based on the theories of Ainslie Meares, author of *Relief without Drugs* and *Cancer: Another Way*, who both treated and inspired Gawler. The Gawler Foundation (originally the Melbourne Cancer Support Group, subsequently the Australian Cancer Patients Foundation) of which Ian Gawler was Therapeutic Director for thirty years, is a nonprofit organisation which promotes self-help techniques for cancer sufferers and their families based on meditation, stress-management, diet change and relaxation. Over twelve thousand cancer sufferers have used the services of the Foundation, with over fifty thousand attending various programs for healthy living.

Gawler is the author of many publications, the best-known of which is possibly the first: *You Can Conquer Cancer*. He also leads outback excursions with a special focus on meditation. Ian Gawler was awarded the OAM in 1987 in recognition of his work. *Ian Gawler: The Dragon's Blessing* by Guy Allenby was published in 2008. In 2011 *Internal Medicine* published a paper suggesting that Gawler's tuberculosis may have been misdiagnosed as cancer, which Gawler has rebutted.

ری

William Ralph Boyce Gibson (1869–1935)

When Boyce Gibson accepted the chair of Mental and Moral Philosophy at the University of Melbourne in 1911 he already had considerable achievements behind him, having lectured in English universities, written books on ethics, logic and the philosophy of Eucken, and published in journals, including the *Proceedings* of the Aristotelian Society, London, *Mind* and the *Revue de métaphysique et de morale.*

He espoused the tenets of Personal Idealism, a belief in the metaphysical autonomy of personality, as opposed to both Naturalism, which considers personality an outcome of 'the mechanism of Nature', and Idealism which considers it an 'adjective' of the Absolute. In 1906 and 1909 Gibson published works on Eucken's interpretation of Personal Idealism which held, as Gibson expressed it, that 'the measure and standard of our thought is fixed by the measure and standard of our life'.

Gibson's interest in the work of Henri Bergson and the relation of physics and philosophy informed his presidential address to the 1931 conference of the Australian Association for the Advancement of Science, entitled 'Relativity and First Principles'. He was also deeply interested in the Phenomenological movement and his translation of Husserl's *Ideen zu einer Phänomenologie und phänomenologischen Philosophie* in 1931 introduced Husserl to Anglophone readers.

Lucy Judge Peacock (1872–1953) married Gibson in 1898. She had studied classics and oriental languages at Girton and Sanskrit at the Sorbonne and Jena. She collaborated with her husband on two translations of the work of Eucken and translated another alone.

The Gibsons had five sons, four of whom graduated from the University of Melbourne. Keith was killed in a climbing accident in 1925, Alexander (1900–72, BA 1920) became the third Professor of Philosophy at the University of Melbourne, Colin (1911–85, BA 1938) became a Unitarian minister, Quentin (1913–2001, BA 1934) established Philosophy at the Canberra University College (later the Australian National University) and Ralph (1906–89, BA 1927) became a leading member of the Australian Communist Party.

Zygmunt Gizycki (1910–2001)

When he arrived in Australia in 1949 under a government scheme to recruit medical practitioners, Dr Zygmunt Gizycki found that the newly elected Menzies administration did not recognise his qualifications. He had graduated from the University of Poznan in 1936 and served in military hospitals on the Eastern Front. When the Polish Front collapsed in 1939, he was briefly imprisoned in Auschwitz-Birkenau. Released without explanation, he was conscripted by the Swiss Red Cross, assisting in the identification of the Polish officers massacred by the Russians in the Katyn forest. At the end of the war, until 1949, he worked in a West German Displaced Persons Camp as a medical officer.

Migration to Australia meant choosing a second profession. Working as a hospital orderly and assistant in a photographic laboratory, Gizycki set about establishing his new career by studying Dentistry at the University of Melbourne. He graduated in 1957 and worked for the Victorian School Dental Service, travelling to country schools for almost twenty years.

Mandatory retirement from this employment at the age of sixty-five saw him embark on a third career, when, sponsored by the Victorian Dairy Association, he lectured to schoolchildren all over the state on diet and dental health, and campaigned for healthier tuckshop foods.

Gizycki's fourth career began in 1988 when, aged seventy-eight, he began lecturing in the Health Sciences at the Laws College of Naturopathy. This work continued until shortly before his death. He was President of the Pritikin Health Association and took an active interest in many other health associations.

Gizycki was a foundation member of both the Polish RSL and Polish Association. An accomplished photographer, he took pictures for the Melbourne Zoo and for the Polly Woodside restoration project, on which he also provided physical assistance.

෴

Pierre Patrick Gorman (1924–2006)

Pierre Gorman was born in Melbourne to Sir Eugene and Marthe Gorman. He attended Melbourne Church of England Grammar School and the University of Melbourne, taking the degrees of BAgSci and BEd in 1949 and 1951 before proceeding to Cambridge University, where he graduated PhD in 1960. A normal enough education for many others, Pierre Gorman's was remarkable because he was born profoundly deaf and was the first such person to take a PhD from Cambridge.

Pierre Gorman (left) and
Sir Edward Woodward, 2000

His career spanned many aspects of the same mission —a determination that people with disabilities, especially, although not exclusively, that of deafness, should be enabled to succeed in the open community. In his occasional address at the University of Melbourne in 2000, following the conferring of the degree LLD *honoris causa*, Pierre Gorman expressed the hope that this would encourage further research 'to determine how negative attitudes and behaviour towards disabilities and their owners can be reduced, or better still, eliminated'.

After graduation from Cambridge, Gorman worked with Sir Richard Paget on the Paget-Gorman sign system, and was appointed as the first information officer of the National Institute for the Deaf, eventually building its library into one of the world's great resources on all aspects of speech and hearing. He followed his leadership of the Policy Investigation Project of the Victorian School for Deaf Children by joining the Faculty of Education at Monash University, retiring in 1983.

At this point Gorman re-established his connection with Melbourne University, offering to the University Library his collection of books and pictorial works related to Cambridge. The original six hundred titles swelled to over three thousand pamphlets, periodicals and monographs on all aspects of Cambridge life.

Some of the pictures may be seen on the walls of the School of Graduate Research in the 1888 Building. This collection represents an extraordinary tribute to Pierre Gorman's happy association with Cambridge University, especially Corpus Christi College. It provides Melbourne scholars with a unique resource.

George Percy Aldridge Grainger (1882–1961)

Percy Grainger's Lot is Hard—
Running Dog of the Avant Garde
He'd rather be, if truth were said
Music's Whipping boy instead.

John Poynter's verse alludes to Percy Grainger's pre-eminent place among composers and to his sexual preferences. Visitors to the Grainger Museum within the University Grounds can find ample evidence of both.

Grainger was a child prodigy who gave public piano performances from the age of twelve, having presented his mother with his first composition a year earlier. At thirteen, he was enrolled in Dr Hoch's Conservatorium in Frankfurt-am-Main. His concert career began in earnest in 1900: he traversed England, South Africa, Europe and Australasia. Recognition of his ability as a composer and conductor came with the Balfour Gardiner Choral and Orchestral Concerts of 1912 and 1913.

In 1914 Grainger left Britain for the United States, a move which alienated some British friends, who were only partially mollified by his joining the US Army as a bandsman. He took American citizenship in 1918.

War's end brought a succession of tours, combined with teaching and composing. 'Country Gardens' was published in 1919. His father (the architect of Melbourne's Princes Bridge) died of syphilis in 1917; his mother's suicide in 1922 deprived him of a constant companion and guide. Grainger met the Swedish-born Ella Viola Ström in 1926: they married in 1928.

His Australian tour for the ABC in 1934–35 profoundly affected the University because the proceeds were devoted to the establishment of the Music Museum and Grainger Museum. 'A Commonsense View of All Music', the twelve radio talks he gave during this period, set out his 'universalist' view of music and admiration for the 'Nordic group' of composers.

Grainger's sexual proclivities and racialist views, together with the runaway popularity of 'Country Gardens', for some time overshadowed his brilliance and originality as a musician. Later recordings of his work re-established him in the Australian musical pantheon.

ᏉᏊ

Michelle Grattan (1944–)

Michelle Grattan is one of Australia's best-known journalists and, when appointed Editor of the *Canberra Times* in 1993, she became the first woman to achieve such a position on a major Australian daily newspaper.

Grattan majored in Political Science, graduating BA in 1966. She tutored in Politics at Monash University before joining the staff of *The Age*, then under the editorship of Graham Perkin. She became Chief Political Correspondent in 1976, the first woman to be appointed to the position. In 1988 she won the Graham Perkin Award as Australian Journalist of the Year.

Michelle Grattan's industry and meticulousness are legendary, as are her late night and early morning telephone calls to members of parliament in order to check stories before they go to press.

Grattan left the *Canberra Times* in 1995, taking senior positions with *The Age* and *Australian Financial Review*. She has also been a frequent commentator on both radio and television and has published several books, either alone or in collaboration, including *Can Ministers Cope? Australian Federal Ministers at Work* (1981), *Managing Government: Labor's Achievements and Failures* (1993) and *Reconciliation: Essays on Australian Reconciliation* (2000). Her published public lectures include the 1988 Arthur Norman Smith Memorial Lecture in Journalism, entitled *Reporting Federal Politics*, and the 1995 Murdoch Memorial Lecture, *Headline, Deadline, Bottom Line: The Case for Good Journalism*. The revised edition of her *Australian Prime Ministers*, originally published in 2000, appeared in 2010.

In 2013 Michelle Grattan left Fairfax after fifty years in the Canberra press corps to take up an honorary position at the University of Canberra and to work on the online newsletter *The Conversation*.

Dimitry Vladimirovich Grishin (1908–75)

In *The Australian People*, James Jupp tells us that many Russian immigrants to Australia after World War II had concealed their origins for fear of being sent from Displaced Persons Camps to live under Stalin. 'Disillusioned and afraid because of real or imagined concerns about their past, many were anxious to start completely afresh and so made few efforts to recover their ethnic identity.'

Dimitry Vladimirovich Grishin, whom Jupp describes as 'a highly respected academic teacher and scholar', exhibited no such tendency. In Nina Christesen's words, 'Remembered for the very Russian atmosphere he created around him, Grishin insisted on speaking his native tongue to those who could understand the language and teaching it to those who could not.'

Grishin had taught Russian literature at Moscow University before the War. In 1942 he and his wife were taken prisoner and sent to Berlin. They escaped to Emden and arrived in Australia in 1949. At the Bonegilla immigrant camp, Grishin organized protests against the living conditions there. He took Australian citizenship in 1954 and began tutoring in Russian at the University while working at Monsanto Chemicals (Australia). By 1970 he had been appointed Reader.

Grishin's research at Moscow University in the 1940s had been on 'Early Dostoyevsky', and his Melbourne PhD, awarded in 1957, was on Dostoyevsky's *Diary of a Writer*. He founded the International Dostoyevsky Society and published extensively on his work.

Both of Grishin's sons graduated from Melbourne University. Vladimir Grishin (1945–) took his MA in 1971 with a thesis on Gogol. Sasha (Alexander) Grishin (1950–), academic and art critic, took his BA (1972) and MA (1975) from Melbourne before moving to the ANU. His thesis was on Stroganov icon-painting and his published books include work on Vadim Sidur, Andrew Sibley, Leonard French and S.T. Gill. He was appointed to the Sir William Dobell Chair in Art History in 2006.

෬෬

Roy Burman Grounds (1905–81)

Roy Grounds pioneered the design of blocks of flats in Australia before the World War II, designed several notable houses, especially in Victoria and the ACT, after he returned from service with the RAAF, and, at the end of his career, was most widely recognised for large public buildings in Melbourne and Canberra. His influence on the University was profound.

Grounds was educated in Melbourne and articled to the firm of Blacketts and Forester. In 1932, an award from the Royal Victorian Institute of Architects enabled him to study in England and the United States. On his return, he formed a partnership with Geoffrey Mewton: two houses from this period were described by the Institute at the time as 'the best house design in Victoria this century'. To this early period also belong several blocks of flats, notable for efficient use of space combined with high aesthetic standards.

After war service with construction units of the RAAF, Grounds resumed practice in 1948, also assisting in developing the curriculum of the University's School of Architecture, where he lectured in Design. At the same time, he took a degree course in Architecture, graduating in 1953.

The houses which Grounds designed during this time are remarkable for their geometric innovation: they include a triangular house in Kew and circular houses in Canberra and Frankston.

His best-known designs, however, are large public buildings, most notably the copper-domed Australian Academy of Science, the National Gallery of Victoria and the St Kilda Road Arts Centre complex. The Shine Dome, housing the Academy of Science in particular, described as 'a beehive for boffins', was intended to reflect and complement the natural setting of the building, with the dome reflecting the hills surrounding Canberra. Previously known as Becker House, it was renamed in 2001 in honour of John Shine (1946–), who is perhaps best known for the Shine-Dalgarno Sequence and winner of the 2010 Prime Minister's Prize for Science. On the Melbourne University campus, Grounds designed the John Medley Building and extensions to Ormond College.

Grounds was awarded the gold medal of the Royal Australian Institute of Architects in 1968 and made a Life Member the following year.

Rupert James Hamer (1916–2004)

When he was a Law student at the University of Melbourne, 'Dick' Hamer and some friends protested at Chamberlain's appeasement of Hitler by putting a homemade gasmask over the face of the statue of Matthew Flinders outside St Paul's Cathedral. During the subsequent War, he served in North Africa, France and New Guinea and was involved in planning the Allied crossing of the Rhine.

Hamer had been admitted to the Bar in 1940, and practised as a solicitor after the War. He joined the Liberal Party in 1946. In 1958 he was elected to the Victorian Parliament, serving as MLC for East Yarra Province until 1971, when he joined the House of Assembly as Member for Kew. He occupied a number of portfolios before succeeding Sir Henry Bolte as Premier in 1972. He resigned in 1981.

Hamer's Premiership signalled an unprecedented involvement by the state government in 'quality of life' matters. In his own words, he believed Government needed to 'introduce into the whole picture the idea that our surroundings were important, that our heritage was important—both natural and manmade—that we needed to look after the environment more and to develop the arts and leisure, including physical relaxation'.

Described by the Labor leader in the Upper House, Jack Galbally, as 'the man who never lost his temper', Hamer was above all a consensus builder.

He was active, both in parliament and after his retirement, in issues which crossed party boundaries, ranging from the anti-hanging campaigns of the 1960s to the campaign for an Australian republic and more humane treatment of asylum seekers. He advocated reform of the Legislative Council.

The range of his interests was evident in his chairmanship at various times of the Victorian State Opera, National Heritage Foundation, Greenhouse Action Australia and the Melbourne International Chamber Music Competition, and membership of many other bodies.

Hamer's sister, Alison Patrick (1921–2009, BA 1942, PhD 1970), was a distinguished specialist in the history of the French Revolution and author of the seminal book, *The Men of the First French Republic* (1972). She was Head of the History Department 1977–80. In 2006 she published *Revolution for Beginners: Reflections on the History of Late-Eighteenth Century France*.

☙

Eleanor Harding (1935–96)

Eleanor Harding was not a graduate of the University of Melbourne, but her determination and encouragement ensured a tertiary education for six of her seven children and many other members of Victoria's Aboriginal community.

Harding came to Melbourne from Queensland in 1956 with her husband. After a short period in South Yarra they moved to Fitzroy, where 'Aunty Eleanor' became a stalwart of the close-knit Aboriginal and white community. Interviewed in the 1980s for the Cutten History Committee of the Fitzroy History Society's *Fitzroy: Melbourne's First Suburb*, she spoke of the desperate situation of black and white neighbours, constrained by uncongenial working hours to leave children to be minded by neighbours, and of her electric toaster doing the rounds of the neighbourhood. 'We had to have breakfast earlier, so others could use the toaster.'

Harding worked for many years with the Victorian Department of Community Services, principally with victims of domestic violence. She was also a mentor for many young people during their school and university years, encouraging and inspiring them to keep going. Two of her own children, Destiny Deacon and John Harding, are Melbourne graduates. Janina Harding graduated from RMIT University, Tom Peterson from La Trobe University and Clinton Nain from Victoria College of the Arts.

Destiny Deacon (1957– , BA 1979, DipEd [LaTrobe] 1981) taught History before devoting herself to photography. She has exhibited widely in Australia and overseas. Her work was placed in the 'Top 50 Australian Art Collectibles' by *Australian Art Collector* in 2002.

John Harding (1961– , BA 1982, GradDipEd 1986) is an award-winning playwright. *Up the Road* won the Kate Challis RAKA Award in 1997. He was awarded the 2002 Nugget Coombs Writing Fellowship at the ANU, and his 2008 documentary *Fitzroy Stars: More Than a Game* aired on ABC TV.

Ernst Johannes Hartung (1893–1979)

Ernst Hartung (left) with George Ampt, c. 1940–42

E.J. Hartung succeeded fellow Wesley Collegian David Rivett as Professor of Chemistry from 1928 to 1953 and during the first years of his term was heavily involved in the design and construction of a new building for the Chemistry School. He served three times as General President of the (Royal) Australian Chemical Institute and represented Australia in 1931 at the centenary meeting of the British Association for the Advancement of Science. Professor Hartung lived with his family on campus in what is now University House.

Having worked on the design of gas masks with Masson and Laby during World War I, Hartung made a notable contribution during the World War II as chairman of the Advisory Committee on Optical Munitions, and produced trial batches of optical glass for use in optical munitions using local raw materials for the crucibles and melts. Large-scale production, based on Hartung's work, was undertaken by Australian Consolidated Industries. British experts had estimated that this would take four years and cost a million pounds, but the Australian team achieved their results in ten months at a cost of £60,000.

Photography was a lifelong interest and Hartung's record of the various forms of Brownian movement in colloidal solution on 35 mm cinefilm was copied for its World Science Library onto 16 mm film by the Eastman Kodak Company. When he took early retirement in 1953, Professor Hartung established an observatory on Lavender Farm at Woodend and in 1968 published *Astronomical Objects for Southern Telescopes: A Handbook for Amateur Observers*, based on his study of some 4000 stellar objects.

The 1983 Ash Wednesday bushfires which destroyed Lavender Farm also consumed Professor Hartung's diary of some 7000 pages. Part of his professional library and other papers are held in the University of Melbourne Archives.

❧

William Edward Hearn (1826–88)

From the perspective of our age of specialisation, W.E. Hearn seems extraordinarily versatile. He was appointed as the University's first Professor of Modern History and Literature, Political Economy and Logic in 1854 and, following the untimely death of the foundation Professor of Classics, he also taught Classics in 1855–56 and 1871. His students included H.B. Higgins, Alfred Deakin and Isaac Isaacs.

In 1873, Hearn was then appointed the first Dean of Law, lecturing in Constitutional Law and Jurisprudence. *The Cassell Prize Essay on the Condition of Ireland* was published in 1851, before his arrival in Australia. In Melbourne he published four more books, which enjoyed local success as well as bringing Australian scholarship to world attention. He was also a prolific journalist, publishing in the *Argus* and *Australasian*.

Hearn was an active Anglican who took great interest in the affairs of Trinity College and the Diocese of Melbourne. His books covered subjects as diverse as political economy, the growth of constitutional law and conventions, early social institutions such as the family and household and, in *The Theory of Legal Duties and Rights*, the theoretical reasoning behind his attempts to codify the laws of Victoria. This code, which occupied his later years, although praised in parliament, was regarded as too abstract by practising lawyers and never adopted. Despite being admitted to the Victorian Bar and appointed as QC in 1886, he rarely practised.

Hearn's first efforts to be elected to the Legislative Assembly were unsuccessful, with the Chancellor, Redmond Barry, persuading the University Council to prohibit professors from standing for parliament. In 1878, having argued that as a Dean he was not subject to this prohibition, Hearn was elected to the Legislative Council, representing the Central Province. He was castigated by *The Age* as a conservative, but respected in practice for his skill in drafting legislation.

☙❧

Bernard Thomas Heinze (1894–1982)

Generations of Melbourne schoolchildren remember excursions to the Melbourne Town Hall for the Young People's Concerts. For many, it was their introduction to classical music. The concerts, which took place in all capital cities, owed their existence to Bernard Heinze, who also established the ABC's Youth Orchestra concerts.

Heinze (MA 1948) won a scholarship from the University of Melbourne to the Royal College of Music, London, in 1912. After five years in the Royal Artillery, followed by studies in Paris and Berlin, he toured Europe as a violinist in a string quartet.

In 1923 he returned to the Melbourne Conservatorium and was appointed Ormond Professor of Music in 1925, a position he held until 1956. Heinze established and conducted the Melbourne University Symphony Orchestra in 1924. In 1933, this merged with Fritz Hart's Melbourne Symphony Orchestra. Heinze remained as its conductor until 1956, when he succeeded Eugene Goossens as Director of the New South Wales Conservatorium. In 1929 Heinze was appointed Director-General of Music at the ABC and established what were to become the State Orchestras, the celebrity concerts and many other programs. He was Life Conductor of the Melbourne Philharmonic Society from 1928.

Heinze promoted Australian composers, incorporating works by Richard Meale, Peter Sculthorpe, Felix Werder and others in the repertoire of orchestras from the 1950s onwards. He also introduced Australian audiences to much new music of the twentieth century, including composers like Shostakovich, Bartók and Walton.

He was the first Australian to be knighted for services to music. He was awarded an honorary Doctorate of Music by the University in 1977. Thirty years earlier, in 1947, the University of British Columbia had granted him the same honour. The citation described him as a 'scholar, teacher, creative artist, who is a powerful agent in keeping his country's music on levels of eminence'.

☙❧

Ronald Frank Henderson (1917–94)

When Ronald Henderson was recruited from Britain in 1962 to set up the Melbourne Institute of Applied Economic and Social Research, he was no stranger to Australia. He had worked as a Visiting Fellow at the ANU and a Visitor at the Reserve Bank. He was already distinguished for his economic research and teaching at Corpus Christi College, Cambridge and research and publication with the National Institute of Economic and Social Research.

The Institute of Applied Economic and Social Research, to which Henderson was appointed as Reader and Director, was physically located within the Faculty of Economics but independent from it, its Advisory Board being members drawn from both within and outside the University. Henderson initiated an ambitious publication program, including the annual Australian Economic Review and monographs on specific research projects.

People in Poverty: A Melbourne Survey by Henderson, Alison Harcourt and R.J.A. Harper was published in 1970, by which time the Institute staff numbered about forty people. In 1972, the Commonwealth Government invited Henderson to chair the National Inquiry into Poverty. He took three years' leave of absence from the University and, characteristically for Henderson, if untypically for such enterprises, the work was completed on schedule. The 'Henderson Poverty Line', which found 10 per cent of Australians living in poverty in 1973, was a benchmark for almost a quarter of a century and later publications, such as *Australian Poverty: Then and Now* by Ruth Fincher and John Nieuwenhuysen, attest to the enduring importance of Henderson's work.

In retirement, from 1979 to 1985, Henderson worked for the Brotherhood of St Laurence and the Victorian Council of Social Services, and, in the words of Hayden Raysmith, 'Ronald's presence at VCOSS added status to the organisation and weight to its arguments.' The National Inquiry had made him conscious of the extent of poverty in Australia and of the political will necessary to remedy it. Henderson put poverty on the national agenda of the Lucky Country. *Ronald Frank Henderson 1917–1994: A Tribute* by Jean and Davis McCaughey was published in 1997.

☙

John Charles Hibberd (1940–)

Jack Hibberd's *Valete* from Newman College was written by John Funder. It foretold an conventional future: 'will almost certainly wind up a professor, house in North Balwyn, smoking tailor-mades, watching television and looking forward to his holidays at Torquay'. Funder was smiling at his friend's likely compromises, for Hibberd's student exploits had been of legendary proportions, hilariously and brilliantly recounted in his 1983 essay in *Memories of Melbourne University.*

Hibberd graduated MB BS from Melbourne University in 1964 and practised medicine from 1965–73 and again from 1986. His name, however, is principally associated with the theatre.

White with Wire Wheels, his first play, was produced at the University in 1967. The same year, La Mama staged his *Three Old Friends* as their inaugural production. 1969 saw the first staging of one of Hibberd's most frequently performed works, *Dimboola*, in which the audience plays the part of wedding guests, welcomed to performances by the principal actors, and offered refreshments as they arrive.

Two companies performed at La Mama: the La Mama Company and the smaller Tribe, which, in 1970, became the Australian Performing Group, including Hibberd, Graeme Blundell and John Romeril, and moved to The Pram Factory. An Australia Council Literature Board Fellowship gave Hibberd the chance to devote himself entirely to writing. *A Stretch of the Imagination* was first performed there in 1972. It, too, has been frequently revived, perhaps most notably by another Melbourne alumnus, Max Gillies.

In 1982, Hibberd founded the Melbourne Writers' Theatre. As well as almost twenty plays, he has published novels and other works. He is married to the award-winning actor Evelyn Krape, known for solo performances in the works of Dario Fo as well as her role in Hibberd's 1976 *A Toast to Melba.*

On its fortieth anniversary in 2007, Susie Dee produced a new season of *White with Wire Wheels* in the Union House Theatre.

සි

Henry Bournes Higgins (1851–1929)

Born in Ireland just two years before the foundation of the University of Melbourne, Henry Bournes Higgins arrived in Australia in 1870. He graduated in Law in 1874 and took his MA two years later. Elected to the Australasian Federal Convention of 1897–99, he was influential in the framing of the Constitution, despite his opposition to Federation and notable for his support of Irish Home Rule and opposition to Australia's involvement in the Boer War. After a brief and controversial career as Member of Parliament, Higgins was appointed a justice of the High Court in October 1906, remaining on the Bench until his death in 1929.

Higgins is best remembered for his Harvester case judgement in 1907, his first case as President of the Commonwealth Court of Conciliation and Arbitration, in which he ruled for the first time on what constituted a fair minimum wage, establishing that a worker 'as a human being in a civilized community' supporting a family of about five persons, was entitled to a daily wage of no less than seven shillings.

Higgins served on the University of Melbourne Council from 1887 to 1923, during which time he supported the full admission of women and a university extension system (the forerunner of today's Community Access Program). In 1904, he donated £1000 for a scholarship which bears his name, for the study of poetry. The exhibition in Greek part I was also named after him, in recognition of a £500 contribution. He was awarded a DLitt from the University in 1922 for *A New Province for Law and Order*.

Devastated by the death in 1916 of his only son, Higgins maintained a close relationship with his niece and later biographer, the writer Nettie Palmer. He was a strong supporter of the *Bulletin* and, in Deakin's words, 'one of the parents; if not the chief parent' of the Commonwealth Literary Fund.

Janet Gertrude (Nettie) Palmer (1885–1964, BA 1909, MA 1912) exercised, with her husband Vance (1885–1959), a strong and lasting influence on Australian culture. Her many publications include *Fourteen Years: Extracts from a Private Journal 1925–1939* (1948), *Henry Bournes Higgins: A Memoir* (1931) and *Henry Handel Richardson: A Study* (1950).

Ming-Zhu Hii (1981–)

Ming-Zhu Hii (BDram 2002) grew up in Hobart in the 1980s. Like many of her contemporaries, she sought to pursue an artistic career on the mainland and found her life transformed when, at the age of eighteen, she enrolled in the Victorian College of the Arts School of Drama, under the direction of Lindy Davies.

Ming-Zhu Hii's recollections of the School bear out its nickname of 'The Monastery': the daily routine for its students ranged from scrubbing the floors with cold water to meditation. She was introduced to and greatly influenced by the work of Heiner Müller, Romeo Castellucci, Pina Bausch and Howard Barker.

An interdisciplinary writer, director, producer and actor, she has since worked extensively as a performer with leading theatre companies as well as in film and television. She has performed with the Melbourne Theatre Company, Playbox and the Melbourne Festival. Before that, her first piece, *Y*, an exploration of identity, art and conflict inspired by the life and work of Yoko Ono, won critical acclaim when performed in 2006 at the Next Wave Festival. In 2009, with her husband, Nicholas Coghlan, she founded The Public Studio (originally called The Melbourne Town Players). Later that year her 'investigation into the racial identification of Australia', *Attract/Repel*, was staged.

Ming-Zhu Hii is a prolific writer, whose work has been published in *The Age*, the independent magazine *Dumbo Feather* and *Real Time*. She is a strong advocate for greater gender equality and representation of cultural diversity across the professional performing arts in Australia. She has built and run several businesses, including an art and design boutique, and worked with individual artists and designers, small businesses and non-profit organisations as a business coach and consultant. She has sat on two Green Room panels and was a founding member of the Australian Women Directors Alliance.

The Public Studio's first film project, *Hey, Wasteland*, began production in 2013.

☙❧

Charles Archibald Brookes Hoadley (1887–1947)

The connection between Scouting and Violet Crumbles is an indirect one: the popular sweet was manufactured by the brother of the future Chief Commissioner of Victoria, Arch Hoadley, and named in honour of their mother's favourite flower.

Hoadley was the tenth of fourteen children. He was a graduate in Mining Engineering and Science from the University of Melbourne, after which he joined Mawson's 1911–13 expedition to Antarctica. Cape Hoadley in Antarctica is named after him. He took his MSc on his return, winning the Caroline Kay Scholarship in Geology.

After a brief period as Senior Lecturer at the Ballarat School of Mines and Industry, he was appointed as the first Principal of Footscray Technical School in 1916. Under his direction, Footscray Tech was to become the largest diploma teaching school in the state system, with its principal vigorously advocating the long-term benefit of keeping boys at school. At the same time he maintained professional links with a local engineering firm and in 1924 travelled to the United States and Europe to investigate technical education there. He was a charismatic teacher whom the painter, William Dargie, described as 'wonderful, a heroic figure'.

Hoadley's involvement with Scouting dated from 1921, and was invigorated during his 1924 study tour by a course at Gilwell, England. As Chief Commissioner of Victoria from 1928 to 1937, Hoadley is credited with revitalising as well as reorganising the Association.

In 1929, the two preoccupations of his working life again intertwined when, visiting England as Commissioner in charge of the Australian contingent to the Jamboree, he represented the Victorian Education Department at a world conference on adult education.

Hoadley had joined the Freemasons in 1915 and when the Baden-Powell Lodge was consecrated in 1930, with Lord Somers, Governor of Victoria as Master, he was its Deputy Master.

Arch Hoadley is commemorated in many buildings and monuments in Footscray and at Gilwell Park in Gembrook, which he had done much to establish.

භ

Judith Maria Horacek (1961–)

The title of Judy Horacek's cartoon exhibition at the National Museum, Canberra, from March to June 2002 was specially apt. *I Am Woman, Hear Me Draw* combines the wit and feminism of her work and hinted at her insistence that cartoons are independent statements rather than accompaniments to written stories.

Horacek took her BA from the University of Melbourne in 1991, following her major in Fine Arts and English with a Diploma of Museum Studies. Her Honours thesis, on the 1930s journal *Manuscripts*, inspired her with the egalitarianism of print-making, making art accessible.

Cartoons published in *Judy's Punch*, the *Legal Service Bulletin* and *Health Issues Centre Journal* led to regular commissions from *Australian Left Review* and *Australian Society* as well as publication in *Meanjin*. Horacek's first commissioned work for *The Age*, published on International Women's Day 1995, next to the obituary of Senator Olive Zakharov, was *Woman with Altitude*, a work which has since appeared on countless fridge doors, greeting cards, tea-towels and t-shirts.

When Horacek began publishing she found that 'the Everyperson in cartoons is traditionally a white, male figure. To make the central character a woman risked people misunderstanding it, because they'd be sure if it had a woman in it, it had to be about childcare or menstruation.' Her cartoons have always been political, being as she says as 'the graphic equivalent of yelling into a megaphone'. Horacek's interest in postmodernism is as distinguishing feature of her work as the clear, clean lines of her drawing.

In recent years, Horacek has produced several bestselling children's books including *Where Is the Green Sheep?* (2004, text by Mem Fox), *The Story of Growl* (2007), *These Are My Feet* (2007), *These Are My Hands* (2009) and *Yellow Is My Favourite Colour* (2010).

Several other members of the Horacek family are Melbourne alumni. Her mother graduated in Science and her father, Ivan Horacek (1935, MB BS 1960), in Medicine. He worked as a Pathologist at the Royal Women's Hospital 1971–92 and taught medical students as a Senior Associate in the Department of Obstetrics and Gynaecology in 1974–92.

☙❧

Alice Hoy (1893–1976)

Alice Hoy did much to shape the future of teacher training in Victoria, and through one of her books—*Civics for
Australian Schools,* published in 1925 and revised almost
annually for the next twenty years—much to shape
Victorian children's knowledge of their political and social
environment.

Born in Ararat, the youngest of eleven children,
she moved to Kensington in 1903. She was educated at
Kensington State School and University High School, from
which she proceeded to the University of Melbourne,
taking her BA in 1914, DipEd in 1915 and MA the
following year.

Alice Hoy was the first person appointed to teach History Method at the Melbourne
Teachers' College in 1924, combining this with an attachment from 1926 to 1958 as Senior
Lecturer in the University's School of Education. After a study tour of Britain and North
America in 1938, she was appointed in 1949 as Principal of the newly established Secondary
Teachers' Training Centre (later College) at the University.

Relations between the University's Department of Education and the College were
not always free of strain, perhaps understandable in the light of Hoy's comments on 'the
lack of clear and orderly presentation in some of our University teaching'. Alice Hoy was
nonetheless a force in almost all aspects of education training and research for almost fifty
years and a notable member of the comparatively small number of women who have shaped
the University. She served on the councils of University Women's College, the Australian
College of Education and Monash University.

A building in Monash Road bears her name, and a portrait of Hoy by Chris White is
held in the Ian Potter Museum of Art.

John Barry Humphries (1934–)

Barry Humphries did not graduate from the University of Melbourne, but few of his undergraduate contemporaries were unaware of his presence among them.

His Dada exhibitions included twisted forks entitled 'Something to Catch the Eye', a gilded jockstrap resting on a velvet cushion labelled 'The Support of Kings' and a custard-filled gumboot identified as 'Pus in Boots'. These attracted as much attention as his lunchtime revue 'Call Me Madman'. His antics on the Alamein train line, where he could empty a crowded carriage by peering at fellow passengers through a hole torn in the newspaper held before his face, were the stuff of student legend.

Humphries left academia for the stage in 1954, performing in the Union Repertory Company production of *The Young Elizabeth*. He subsequently toured in *Twelfth Night* and played Colonel Pickering in Peter O'Shaughnessy's *Pygmalion*, starring Sheila Florance as Eliza.

His most enduringly popular character, Edna Everage, made her first appearance in 1955, together with the stoic and philosophical Sandy Stone, in *A Nice Night's Entertainment*.

Humphries left for England in 1959, a move which inspired the creation of Debbie, the Australian lass in Earl's Court on a working holiday, and Barry McKenzie, the drunken innocent abroad, who was portrayed by Barry Crocker in two films in the 1970s. Other personages of note who appeared in later one-man shows include the idiot intellectual Neil Singleton and venal trade unionist Lance Boyle, as well as the disgusting Sir Les Patterson, Australia's Cultural Attaché to the Court of St James and Chairman of the Australian Cheese Board.

Humphries is a prolific author, and published his first book, *Bizarre*, at the age of twenty-six. His most recent works are the autobiographical *More Please* (1992), *Women in the Background* (1995) and *My Life as Me* (2002). Dame Edna Everage, ennobled by Gough Whitlam in 1974, has produced *Dame Edna's Coffee Table Book* (1976), *Dame Edna's Bedside Companion* (1982) and *Dame Edna: My Gorgeous Life* (1989). *Handling Edna: The Unauthorised Biography* was published in 2009. The University conferred the honorary degree of Doctor of Laws on Barry Humphries in 2006.

☙

Moshi (Mowsey) Inagaki (1880–1947)

Moshi Inagaki was born in Shizuoka Province, Japan, and arrived on Australian shores by boat, landing on Thursday Island and thence in Darwin some time after 1897.

By 1903, he was enrolled in art classes at the National Gallery of Victoria, where he met a strong-minded young school teacher, Rose Allkins. They married in 1907: their daughter, Mura Rose Earle, died in 1989.

The Inagakis were to suffer from their union. Inagaki was refused naturalisation on his marriage and again when he tried to enlist in the AIF in 1915. In 1916 the couple were obliged to register under the War Precautions (Aliens Registration) Regulations and, in 1917, Australian-born Rose Inagaki was struck off the electoral roll.

In 1922, Inagaki became sole instructor in Japanese at Melbourne University. He received no salary, being funded purely through payments from his students. In 1924, the Registrar noted his extraordinary zeal.

The day World War II was declared, the Inagakis tried to register as aliens at their local Police Station, but were told it was unnecessary. On 8 December 1941, however, Rose Inagaki returned from work to find the house ransacked and her husband missing. He had been taken to Tatura Internment Camp without even being permitted to leave her a note. Japanese dictionaries, books and a typewriter had been removed, together with almost twenty pounds in cash. In Tatura, Inagaki was to meet a former student, 'Monte' Punshon, an interpreter for the Australian Army and warden at the camp.

Rose Inagaki pleaded with the University to intervene on behalf of her husband, telling Sir John Latham, 'He has honoured and trusted Australia and never doubted that he would receive fair and just treatment from Australia in any circumstances. He has given 23 years or more quiet unassuming service to the Melbourne University.'

The Registrar expressed sympathy, but noted that 'Mr Inagaki was not a member of its regular staff'. Rose Inagaki died in 1943. Her husband returned to Japan after the war, and died in 1947.

☙❧

Isaac Alfred Isaacs (1855–1948)

The pen-portrait of Australia's first native-born Governor-General in the *Australian Dictionary of Biography*, by Zelman Cowen, reveals a man of contradictions. A fierce supporter of the White Australia Policy, Isaac Isaacs nonetheless prided himself on speaking some Chinese as well as several European languages. No socialist, he nevertheless conceded the necessity of state intervention to achieve decent wages and conditions.

Isaacs was born in Melbourne, moving to Yackandandah at the age of four and Beechworth a few years later. His father was a tailor. After teaching at local schools, he entered the Crown Law Department, studying Law part-time at Melbourne University from 1876. Isaacs used to begin studying at 4 a.m. in order to keep his full-time job. He was a brilliant student, with exceptional recall, and graduated in minimum time, taking his LLM in 1883.

In 1890 he appeared before the Full Supreme Court no fewer than nineteen times. His capacity for hard work, which later led Sir Robert Garran to comment that, 'By day he carried on the biggest practice of the Victorian Bar; by night he did full justice to the duties of Attorney-General', was evident from the first.

Isaacs was first elected to the Victorian Legislative Assembly from the seat of Bogong, which included his childhood towns of Yackandandah and Beechworth. A fervent supporter of Federation, he stepped down as Premier of Victoria to win the federal seat of Indi. In 1905, he was appointed Attorney-General. In 1906, he was appointed to the High Court of Australia, where he served for almost a quarter of a century.

In 1931, Isaacs was appointed Governor-General. He retired in 1936. During these years of Depression, Isaacs voluntarily gave up a quarter of his salary and refused the judge's pension to which he was entitled.

Towards the end of his life, Isaacs caused consternation in the Jewish community by his opposition to 'political Zionism' and his *ad hominem* attacks on those who opposed British policy in Palestine. He is remembered, nonetheless, as a jurist who believed in the courts as 'living organs of a progressive community' and worked always to improve social conditions.

☙

Percy Jones (1914–92)

Percy Jones came from a musical family. His father was bandmaster of the St Augustine's Orphanage Band at the age of sixteen and, in 1925–27, in charge of the Geelong West Band. He taught music at both Geelong Grammar and Geelong College. Three of his five children had musical careers. Dorothea was a singer, Basil a violinist and Director of the Queensland Conservatorium of Music, and his eldest son was destined to become Australia's foremost liturgical musician.

Jones's studies for the priesthood after 1930 were undertaken in Rome, with the intention of fitting him to take responsibility for music in the Melbourne Diocese. His musical talents had already attracted the attention of Percy Grainger at the Conservatorium. Ordained in 1937, he was appointed Music Director at St Patrick's Cathedral in 1942. He occupied this position for thirty-one years. From 1950 to 1972 he was also Vice-Director of the Conservatorium, a title he especially enjoyed using in conjunction with his clerical collar.

During the 1940s, Jones began collecting Australian folksongs. Without a tape-recorder this involved transcribing words and music from live performance. 'Click Go the Shears' and 'Botany Bay' were thus collected and published in *Australian Bush Songs* by Jones and Burl Ives. In 1942, Jones also published his *Australian Hymnal*, later replaced by his *Pius X Hymnal*.

During the 1950s, he was a driving force in the establishment of the Victorian Schools Music Association, the National Music Camp Association and the Australian Youth Orchestra. During the 1960s, he was a member of the Liturgy Commission of the Second Vatican Council. On his retirement in 1979, he was made a Foundation Fellow of the Melbourne College of Divinity, in recognition of his contribution to the Ecumenical Movement.

Percy Jones was also, in the words of his biographer Donald Cave, part of 'an academically ecumenical group noted for the love of good humour, good conversation, and, to the scandal of not a few, good wine'.

Vahram Nazareth Tacvor Karagheusian (1898–1968)

Nazar Karagheusian finished teaching at the end of 1956, but his personality lives on in the Karagheusian Room of University House, lavishly furnished in walnut in the Renaissance-revival style of nineteenth-century France. The furniture, presented by Karagheusian and his sister Elza Ispénian, originally graced their Paris flat.

'Kara' was a larger-than-life character, a teacher remembered as much for his personality as for the love of his subject which he instilled in his students. Parisian by birth and Armenian by descent, Karagheusian had travelled to Australia with the tennis player Aslangul and stayed on, first going into business and then taking up a vacant position in the Department of French in 1923.

He greatly fostered the social side of University life. Under his guidance, French Club activities attracted groups of two hundred students, schoolchildren and adult francophiles. Large groups of students accompanied him on walks around Healesville, the Dandenongs and Kinglake, observing his rule that French was to be spoken at all times.

In December 1939, Karagheusian was among the first from the University to enlist in the AIF, serving in the Middle East and New Guinea between 1940 and 1943. A weak heart ended his military career in 1944 and he resumed teaching in 1945.

After the war, many students benefited from the travel grants he established in memory of his mother, using her maiden name of Marie Aghassian. He was a notable benefactor of the Armenian churches of both Sydney and Melbourne.

Karagheusian is remembered by his students and colleagues as a man rarely seen without a book in his hand. Colleague Stan Scott described him as 'a tireless emissary and embodiment of French life and culture, an impressive if unorthodox teacher, and from the start, a source of animation throughout the faculty'. Former student Bill Hannan remembered of the early 1950s that 'Kara' 'conducted exams in his bungalow in the hills and served chicken and brandy as the students toiled'.

ख

William Charles Kernot (1845–1909)

William Kernot, the first qualified engineer to be produced by the University of Melbourne and its foundation Professor of Engineering, was obliged to defend himself at the 1902–04 Royal Commission on the University against accusations of superficiality and lack of mathematical and analytical rigour in his lectures. There was evidence, however, that he could be equally devastating in response.

Kernot entered the University at fifteen, graduating with an MA and Certificate of Civil Engineering in 1866. From 1865 to 1875 he was unhappily employed in various Victorian government departments, declaring, as Stephen Murray-Smith informs us in the *Australian Dictionary of Biography*, that his colleagues 'were perfectly unconscious even of the existence of physical laws'.

He was employed part-time at the University before being appointed Professor of Engineering in 1882, the first alumnus to be awarded a Chair. As well as teaching for twenty-three hours a week, Kernot undertook significant contracts and consultancies. He chaired two prize juries and was a member of a third for the International Exhibition of 1880. He reported to the Tasmanian government on railway bridges in the Derwent Valley and the Victorian government on placing telephone and telegraph wires underground. He was a member of the 1884 NSW Royal Commission on Railway Bridges.

The University was not Kernot's sole concern. He was active in professional organisations, chaired the Royal Society of Victoria from 1885 to 1900 and the Council of the Working Men's College, with which he retained a lifelong involvement, from 1889. Both College and University benefited from his generosity. He provided £2000 for University scholarships in Physics and Chemistry in 1887, £200 for one in Geology in 1908 and £1000 for a metallurgical laboratory. To the College he gave £300 for a foundry in 1893, followed by £300 in 1901. In 1886 he won bipartisan acclaim for his chairmanship of the Board of Arbitrators in the waterfront strike. As Chairman of Directors of the New Australian Electricity Co., he brought electric lighting to Melbourne.

Despite criticism of his teaching at the later Royal Commission, Kernot is recognised as having laid strong foundations for Engineering at the University of Melbourne.

Margaret Loch Kiddle (1914–58)

Margaret Kiddle was fourth generation Australian, an inheritance which was to serve her well in her research for the work which made her reputation.

She was a born teacher, but unable to work in a school because of her poor health: instead she accepted a tutorship, expressing the hope that she would not 'be a nuisance to the others by getting sick too often'. She interrupted this work and her MA during World War II, working as Research Assistant to Douglas Copland in his work on prices policy. Her thesis on Caroline Chisholm was completed in 1947 and formed the basis of a biography published in 1950, with a second edition in 1957. An abridged edition was published in 1990.

Kiddle and her colleague Kathleen Fitzpatrick were the earliest scholars to publish Australian histories in which women's experience was central. In more recent times, a publisher who was offered *Men of Yesterday: A Social History of the Western District of Victoria, 1834–1890* might recommend a change of main title. It was, however, a quotation which by no means reflects the scope of the work. Into her narrative of a society created by white men, 'almost exclusive of women and concerned almost wholly with work', Kiddle wove women's lives and work, showing their enormous social impact on all aspects of Western District life.

Kiddle's research relied heavily on letters and diaries, which her family connection made easier of access than other scholars might have found them. Nothing, however, could slow the progress of the kidney disease which killed her. She completed revisions to the manuscript in hospital, leaving her literary executors to see them through and make changes as they saw fit. Examination of the typescript shows that she left them little to do.

Men of Yesterday stands as a monument in Australian historical writing. Kiddle's generosity in bequeathing the royalties to the History Department funds the essay prize which bears her name. *Women Historians and Women's History: Kathleen Fitzpatrick (1905–1990), Margaret Kiddle (1914–1958) and the Melbourne History School* by Jane Carey and Patricia Grimshaw was published in 2001.

❧

Frank Knopfelmacher (1923–95)

In his obituary of Frank Knopfelmacher in *The Australian* headed 'Cold War Combatant of the Right', Warren Osmond recalled that 'permanent debate and polemics was his lifestyle of choice'. Other writers refer to his life as a war, a crusade or a fight. He was, throughout over thirty years at the University of Melbourne, one of its best known and most controversial figures.

Frank Knopfelmacher was born in Vienna and brought up in Czechoslovakia. Virtually all his family died in the Holocaust. Having fled to Palestine and subsequently served in a Czech Legion of the British Army, Knopfelmacher returned home in 1948 only to flee once again, this time from the repression following the communist takeover of his country. He went to Britain, taking his PhD from London University. In 1955, he was appointed to the Melbourne University Department of Psychology, where he taught until his retirement in 1988. He reached a wider audience through his lectures on social theory at the Council for Adult Education. He revisited Czechoslovakia only once, in 1990.

Knopfelmacher is remembered by many as a great teacher, whose lectures on complex theoretical issues were models of lucidity. He published extensively, although he produced no single sustained philosophical or sociological work. His output was in journalism and essays addressing the central certainty of his public life—that Nazism and communism were morally indistinguishable and equally evil. His vehement anticommunism, often expressed in provocative language, won him many enemies and, he believed, cost him an appointment as senior lecturer at the University of Sydney. His support of Australian involvement in the Vietnam War further added to his controversial status.

Knopfelmacher attacked what he saw as a failure of Australian academia to develop a specifically Australian understanding of society. His formal and informal teaching brought a new cosmopolitanism to the Australian political debate, even if his polemic was unacceptable to many.

Laby Family

Two generations of the Laby family were intimately involved with Physics at the University. Thomas Howell Laby (1880–1946) overcame pecuniary disadvantage to win an Exhibition of 1851 Science Research Scholarship in 1905, which enabled him to study at the Cavendish Institute. From Cambridge, he was appointed Professor of Physics at Victoria University, Wellington, moving in 1915 to the Melbourne Chair of Natural Philosophy.

Laby's work was crucial in several aspects of Australian science. During World War I he collaborated in the design of valves for an anti-gas respirator. In the 1920s, he (with E.O. Hercus) succeeded in determining the precise equivalent of heat. He worked on the use of radium in cancer therapy and was Commonwealth Adviser in radium from 1929 to 1935. During World War II, Laby chaired the Optical Munitions Panel until 1944.

Laby had supported the appointment of Copland as Vice-Chancellor against Medley and relationships between the two were never easy. He also resigned from a number of organisations such as CSIR, the Australian Radio Research Board and the Australian Institute of Physics over issues of policy and principle. The Physics Department which he headed until 1942 was, however, according to Mark Oliphant, 'by far the best in the Southern Hemisphere'.

Jean Elizabeth Laby (1915–2008) worked with her father on the Optical Munitions Panel. She was a pioneer in architectural drawing classes in the School of Engineering, but her name was omitted from the roll call because she was the only woman. She was appointed Senior Lecturer at the RAAF Academy, Point Cook, in 1961, a position she occupied until 1982. During the 1970s she collaborated on the Climate Assessment Program of the US Department of Transportation, funded by the Office of Naval Research and undertaken with the University of Wyoming.

Her sister, Eudora Betty Laby (1920–), also worked on the Optical Munitions Panel and embarked on a career in statistics, working at the University, the British Tabulating Machine Company, CSIRO and Alcoa. She was awarded an honorary M Sc in 1985.

☙❧

John Michael Landy (1930–)

John Landy, Governor of Victoria from 2001 to 2006, is perhaps best known for almost 'throwing' a race. During the 1956 Australian Mile Championship, he turned back to assist fellow-runner Ron Clarke, who had fallen, which probably cost him a world record. He still went on to win the race, earning a permanent place in the annals of Australian sportsmanship as well as in Australian sport. His action won him the honour of reading the Olympic oath at the 1956 Games in Melbourne.

Olympians from left: *Ralph Doubell, Herb Elliott, John Landy and Merv Lincoln, 2 December 1992*

The photograph of Landy leaping over Clarke prone on the track, taken by fellow athlete Albie Thomas, has become emblematic of sportsmanship. A statue commemorating Landy's gallantry is located in Olympic Park.

Landy was one of the first athletes trained by Percy Cerutty. Training included long runs over sand dunes, year-round swimming and a diet including huge quantities of wheat-germ. He was the second person, and in 1954 the first Australian, to run a mile in under four minutes. He won the bronze medal for the men's 1500 metre race in the 1956 Olympic Games.

John Landy graduated in Agricultural Science in 1954 and developed a particular interest in butterflies. After a year teaching at Geelong Grammar (his own Alma Mater) in 1957, he worked as a Technical Officer with the National Parks Authority and for ICI Australia. He was Chairman of the Wool Research and Development Corporation and of the Victorian Coode Island Review Panel, reviewing options for relocating the chemical storage facility after the disastrous explosion of 1991. He served on the Land Conservation Council of Victoria in 1971–78.

Landy's interest in natural history found expression in two books. The first, *Close to Nature: A Naturalist's Diary of a Year in the Bush*, won the C.J. Dennis award in 1988. The second, *A Coastal Diary*, was published to critical acclaim in 1993. Landy's Field, Geelong's major athletic facility, is named in his honour.

❧

Phillip Garth Law (1912–2010)

Of all the Antarctic expeditioners associated with the University of Melbourne none is better known than Phillip Law. Born in Tallangatta, Victoria, Law was a secondary school teacher from 1929 to 1938, completing his BSc and MSc in Physics part-time between 1939 and 1941. During the war years, he was secretary to the Optical Munitions Panel.

Law was invited to join the 1947–48 expedition of Australian National Antarctic Expeditions (ANARE) to Macquarie Island and Antarctica, and in 1949 became Director of the Antarctic Division of the Commonwealth Department of External Affairs and Leader of ANARE. He persuaded the Australian government to charter the Danish ship *Kista Dan*, which enabled the establishment of permanent stations in Antarctica. Between 1949 and 1966 Mawson, Davis and Casey bases were set up and Law led expeditions which mapped some 4500 kilometres of the Antarctic coastline. He chaired the Australian National Committee on Antarctic Research from 1966 to 1980.

In addition to his role in Australia's Antarctic research, Law contributed to Australian education policy as a member of the Councils of Melbourne and La Trobe Universities, the Victorian Institute of Colleges and the Victorian Institute of Marine Sciences.

In 1960 he was awarded the Founder's Gold Medal of the Royal Geographical Society, an accolade he shares with Livingstone, Burton and Mawson. He was also the recipient of the James Cook Medal of the Royal Society of Victoria and of the Gold Medal of the Australian Geographical Society.

In 1961 his wife Nellie Isobel Law (1925–90), a professional writer and painter, became the first Australian woman to visit Antarctica. In accordance with their wishes, the ashes of Nel and Phillip Law were placed in a cairn at Mawson Station on 19 June 2011.

❧

Leeper Family

Alexander Leeper (1848–1934) was appointed Principal of Trinity College, the first college affiliated with the University, in 1876. Women were admitted to College lectures in 1883. In 1886, separate accommodation was provided for them. Relations between the Council of what became Janet Clarke Hall and that of Trinity were initially strained, and Leeper's relations with Trinity students were at times no better. During one controversy in 1890 he was burned in effigy and two-thirds of the student body left the College.

From left: *Molly, Valentine and Geoffrey Leeper*

Leeper was instrumental in the establishment of Melbourne Church of England Girls Grammar School and a member of its Council as well as that of Melbourne Grammar. He strenuously opposed the reappointment of Marshall-Hall as Ormond Professor of Music, on the grounds of immorality, and his devotion to the British Empire inspired both his opposition to Irish Home Rule and his campaign in the University Council for the dismissal of German members of staff in 1915. He vigorously supported many causes, such as military conscription and the ordination of women.

Warden of Trinity for over forty years, Leeper served almost thirty on the University Council. In retirement, he worked for the Public Library, Museums and National Gallery. The great library he had collected at Trinity carries his name.

Leeper's two sons from his first marriage, Alexander Wigram Allen Leeper (1887–1935, BA 1907) and Reginald Wildig Allen Leeper (1888–1968, BA 1909), had distinguished diplomatic careers in Australia and Britain. From his second marriage, Geoffrey Winthrop Leeper (1903–1986, BSc 1924, MSc 1926) worked in the University's Department of Agriculture from 1934 and was Professor of Agricultural Chemistry from 1962 to 1969. He was President of the Royal Society of Victoria 1959–60 and an Honorary Life Fellow of the Royal Australian Chemical Institute.

Valentine Alexa Leeper (1900–2001, BA 1922), also from his second marriage, was active in classical scholarship and public affairs. She taught History at Saint Margaret's School, Berwick, served as a member of the Council of the League of Nations Union from 1928 to 1945 and took a lifelong interest in Trinity College. Beatrice Mary (Molly) Leeper (1901–92) painted and sang as well as working with the Victoria League, the English Speaking Union and, with her sister, the Classical Association, also a lifelong interest of their father.

☙❧

Brian Bannatyne Lewis (1906–91)

Brian and Miles Lewis

Brian Lewis is remembered for the buildings he designed, including University House at the Australian National University, the Australian headquarters of Penguin Books in Ringwood and Tasmania's Risdon Gaol. At the University of Melbourne his presence was felt in both the structure and content of the degree course in Architecture and the building in which it was long taught.

When Lewis took his DipArch from Melbourne in 1928, the course was taken in the School of Engineering. When he completed it, with brilliant results, he travelled to England, working en route in Malaya and Singapore. His work in Britain won several awards and his drawings were exhibited on three occasions during the 1930s at the Royal Academy. In 1940 he quit the Architectural Department of the Great Western Railway to join the AIF. After service in Syria, North Africa and Australia, he was recruited to the British Ministry of War Transport in 1943 and appointed Chief Architect of the Great Western Railway the following year. In 1946, he took up the Foundation Chair in Architecture at Melbourne University.

A full-time degree course was established, and Lewis assembled a team of notable practitioners to teach it, including Roy Grounds, Fritz Janeba and Robin Boyd. The course emphasised both imaginative design and a solid grasp of structural theory. Many students came from Asia and returned to establish schools of architecture in their own countries. Others took up Chairs in Australia.

Lewis personally organised the building appeal to provide premises for the School, which was at the time housed in a collection of army huts. Gifts came from building contractors, alumni and the allied trades, which provided many of the actual materials. This building, recognised for some time as no longer adequate, was demolished in 2012. The replacement of the building on the same site provided an opportunity to add to the Faculty's history of research through practice.

Brian Lewis was a much-loved teacher, especially valued by overseas students far from home. In retirement, he became a successful painter and the author of two highly regarded autobiographical works: *Sunday at Kooyong Road* (1976) and *Our War* (1981).

His son, Miles Bannatyne Lewis (1943– , PhD 1973), is a well-known teacher, architectural historian and critic of Australian and European architecture. His *Architectura* (2008) has been translated into six languages.

❧

Lorna Lloyd-Green (1910–2002)

Lorna Lloyd-Green graduated in Medicine from the University of Melbourne in 1933. She was to practise as an obstetrician and gynaecologist for fifty years, later re-training and practising for ten years more as a music therapist.

Lloyd-Green held a variety of positions at the Queen Victoria Hospital from 1939 and was Honorary Consultant from 1969 to 1985. She was a pioneer in many issues involving rights of patients and doctors. In 1969 she became the first woman Fellow of the Australian Medical Association and campaigned vigorously for equal pay for female medical staff. She established, and for twenty-five years ran, the infertility clinic which was to become the Monash IVF Clinic.

Active in many women's organisations, both professional and general, Lloyd-Green was President of the Australian Federation of Medical Women and the Medical Women's International Association, a charter member and President of Zonta and a founding member of the Council of St Hilda's College, of which she was also a notable benefactor.

She was the first medical adviser to the Nursing Mothers' Association, now the Australian Breastfeeding Association, and was renowned for never missing a delivery. This devotion to duty led her to spend every night of World War II at the Queen Victoria Hospital, on occasions snatching only a few hours' sleep between births.

When she retired from her obstetrics and gynaecology practice in 1983, Lloyd-Green re-trained as a music therapist, working for almost ten years at Lovell House and Bethlehem Hospice, occasionally charged with selecting music to play to dying women whom she had delivered decades earlier.

Lloyd-Green was a committed Christian. She served on the vestry and as church-warden of St John's Anglican Church, Toorak, and was heavily involved in ecumenical activities.

Lodewyckx/Lodewycks Family

Axel Lodewycks

Augustin Lodewyckx (1876–1964) was born in Belgium and came to Australia after a career which included teaching French and German at the Victoria College, Stellenbosch, South Africa, and educational administration in the Katanga Province, of what was then the Belgian Congo. When he arrived in Melbourne in 1914, he and his family were actually en route for America, but were stranded by the outbreak of war.

Lodewyckx was appointed lecturer in German in 1915 and Associate Professor in 1922. For the next twenty-five years, he not only fostered the development of German within the University and the community at large, but also initiated and supported teaching and research in Dutch, Old Icelandic and Swedish, in some cases writing the textbooks as well as giving the lectures. He published very widely on philology, demography and the history of Germanic languages.

His son, K.A. (Axel) Lodewycks (1910–91), enrolled at the University of Melbourne in 1928, simultaneously working at the Public Library of Victoria (now the State Library). He graduated in 1933 and a six-month overseas trip visiting libraries in Europe and the United States found him in Nuremberg on the Night of the Long Knives. He enlisted in the second AIF in 1940 and served as an intelligence officer and archivist. Lodewycks joined the University Library staff in 1948 and was University Librarian from 1956 to 1973, overseeing the design of the Baillieu Library, in its day an example of cutting-edge architecture. It was the first purpose-built Australian university library for decades.

Relations between Axel Lodewycks and the University administration were frequently acrimonious as he insisted that funding for staff and collections was less than adequate to the needs of the growing institution. During this period, however, the foundations of a great collection were laid, with acquisitions such as the Poynton Collection achieving international importance.

☙

Peter MacCallum (1885–1974)

Peter MacCallum left school in Christchurch, New Zealand, at the age of twelve to work in an ironmonger's store. Australia is fortunate that, as J.S. Guest tells us in the *Australian Dictionary of Biography*, 'His health suffered and, on medical advice, he resumed his schooling.' After working his passage to Britain as a coal-trimmer, MacCallum obtained first-class honours in most subjects in his medical course at Edinburgh University and a double blue for athletics and rugby.

He served with distinction in World War I, winning the Military Cross, and was twice mentioned in dispatches before being gassed and evacuated to England. He married in 1919 and returned with his wife, who lectured in Botany, to lecture in Pathology in Edinburgh. In 1924 he was offered Chairs in Johannesburg and Melbourne and accepted the latter. His arrival signalled a new direction for the life sciences in Melbourne, where the Professors of Pathology, Anatomy and Physiology had occupied their positions for several decades.

MacCallum was more distinguished for his administrative talents than for research, but in fostering such people as F.L. Apperley, E.S.J. King and R.D. 'Pansy' Wright, he created an exceptional research environment. He was President of the University Sports Union and Chairman of the Grounds Committee. During World War II he raised and commanded the Medical Wing of the Melbourne University Rifles; afterwards he chaired the Committee for Post-war Reconstruction, assisting ex-Service personnel wishing to undertake University study.

From 1946 to 1963 MacCallum chaired the Executive Committee of the Anti-Cancer Council. In 1949 he was one of those instrumental in the establishment of the Victorian Cancer Institute and in 1950 its outpatient sections were named the Peter MacCallum Clinic. The 'Peter Mac' housed Australia's first training school for radiotherapists and is a world leader in cancer treatment and research.

The MacCallum family lived in the University grounds for many years, and Monica MacCallum (1921–), Peter's daughter, taught for many years in the Department of History and Philosophy of Science, specialising in the study of Charles Darwin.

McCaughey Family

John Davis McCaughey (1914–2005) came to Melbourne from Northern Ireland as Professor of New Testament Studies in 1953. In 1959 he became Master of Ormond College, a position he occupied for twenty years. He served several terms as a member of Council and as Deputy Chancellor. From 1986 to 1992 he was Governor of Victoria. McCaughey also served from 1961 to 1975 on the Faith and Order Commission of the World Council of Churches. He published several books, including *Victoria's Colonial Governors, 1839–1900* (1993) and *Tradition and Dissent* (1996). A fine biography, *Davis McCaughey: A Life*, by Sarah Martin, was published in 2012.

Jean Middlemas McCaughey (1917–2012) was a social researcher and convenor of People Together. She was a Research Fellow of the Institute for Applied Economic and Social Research from 1966 to 1976 and a board member of the Brotherhood of St Laurence from 1980 to 1990. She chaired the Key Centre for Women's Health in Society and served on the boards of the Royal Melbourne Hospital and St Hilda's College. Her publications include *Where Now? Homeless Families in the Nineties* (1992) and *A Bit of a Struggle: Coping with Family Life in Australia* (1987). In 1997 Jean and Davis McCaughey published *Ronald Frank Henderson, 1917–1994: A Tribute* and in 2009 Jean was awarded an LLD.

The McCaugheys' sons, all Arts graduates of Melbourne University, have established careers in the arts. James McCaughey is a theatre and film director, who established the Theatre Project and the Mill Theatre. John McCaughey is Director of the Astra Chamber Music Society and won an Australian Music Centre Award in 2000 for the most distinguished contribution to the presentation of Australian composition by an individual.

Patrick McCaughey taught at Monash University after a period of art criticism at *The Age* and became Director of the National Gallery of Victoria from 1981 to 1987, a period notable for several blockbuster exhibitions. For eight years he was Director of the Wandsworth Atheneum in Hartford, Connecticut and subsequently became Director of the Yale Center for British Art, resigning this position in 2001 to undertake research and writing. He was awarded an LLD in 2012.

Brigid McCaughey is a primary school teacher specialising in Reading Recovery, an early intervention program for first graders with reading difficulties. Mary McCaughey Nicholson, also a Melbourne University Arts graduate, teaches Italian in primary school.

Henry McCloskey (1891–1952)

Henry McCloskey was the eldest of eight children. He came to the University of Melbourne because the loss of a leg and other wounds had left him unable to resume employment as a plumber at the end of World War I. He was one of the original ANZACs, rose to the rank of Staff Captain and was awarded the Military Cross.

McCloskey's appointment to the position of second laboratory assistant in the Zoology Department, in his own words, 'opened up a new world' to him. He replaced William Mann as Head Laboratory Assistant and the Department

Henry McCloskey and family, c. 1930

came to rely solidly on his industry and competence, especially for the way he set out its Zoological Museum.

He was a foundation member and first Victorian President of the Society of Laboratory Technicians of Australia, a body which sought to improve the training and standing of technical officers. In 1956, this became the Australasian Institute of Medical Laboratory Technologists.

Despite his World War I injuries, McCloskey served as Adjutant at Royal Park, with the rank of Major, during World War II. He received an Efficiency Decoration in recognition of his services.

Although Henry McCloskey did not receive a university education, he was determined that his children should not miss out. Gregory McCloskey (1921–93) was an orthopaedic surgeon; Bertram Payne McCloskey (1923–2007) was known for his research into poliomyelitis. Henry John McCloskey (1925–2000), was Professor of Philosophy at La Trobe University: his *John Stuart Mill: A Critical Study* was published in 1971.

One of McCloskey's daughters-in-law, Mary McCloskey (1923–), was a member of the staff of the Philosophy Department from 1955 to 1988. She took her PhD from Melbourne in 1955. Although he did not live to see her graduate, Henry McCloskey had provided for the purchase of her doctoral gown in his will.

❧

Frederick McCoy (1817–99)

The final paragraph of the entry by G.C. Fendley in the *Australian Dictionary of Biography* for one of the first men appointed Professor in the University of Melbourne paints the portrait of an interesting man: 'Fiery, impulsive, resilient, unsuited to collective enterprises, proud of his robustness, smart in dress, McCoy was of medium height with waved reddish hair, side whiskers and a determined chin. He retained in old age his verve, his jaunty step and his capacity for geniality.'

By the time McCoy came to the University in 1855 as Professor of Natural Science he had already made his name as a palaeontologist and museum director. At the time of his appointment he was Professor of Geology and Mineralogy and Curator of the museum at Queen's College, Belfast. His teaching methods were theoretical rather than practical, depending on classroom exposition rather than field work.

McCoy's chief interest was in museums and, having carried the entire collection of the Government Museum to his rooms in 1856, he was gazetted to the unpaid position of Director of the Museum of Natural and Applied Sciences the following year. A protracted battle for the construction of a museum within the University grounds was won in 1862 and the building (which after his death became the Student Union) opened in 1864, ushering in a period of ceaseless battles with government over funding.

Despite his academic distinction and many honours, McCoy's judgment was not infallible. His enthusiasm for the introduction of exotic species and lack of interest in Aboriginal artefacts reflected a cavalier attitude towards the Australian environment. He was also disastrously inaccurate in identifying gold-bearing land, declaring in 1856 that deep reefs would not be found. He was also a convinced anti-Darwinist, insisting that there was geological proof of the Genesis phases of creation.

McCoy served on numerous government bodies and was a staunch supporter of technical education in Victoria. His reports for the Victorian Board of Science ranged from mining machinery to the use of camels.

ↁ

John Henry MacFarland (1851–1935)

Despite a brilliant school and university career in Northern Ireland as a mathematician, John MacFarland, later Master of Ormond College and University administrator, published nothing either as a mathematical scholar or as an educationist. His influence on education in Australia was, nonetheless, profound.

John MacFarland (right) with the Duke of York, later King George VI, 1927

Francis Ormond had recommended MacFarland's appointment to the College, praising his 'high personal character' and noting that he was a gentlemen, a scholar, and had 'good appearance and pleasing manners'. He was to prove an exceptional administrator who appointed distinguished scholars to his staff and encouraged self-government in the College through its students' club. He was reputed to be severe, often presenting his judgements with exemplary brevity—simply 'yes' or 'no'.

MacFarland was Master of Ormond from 1881 to 1914 and joined the University Council in 1886. He was to serve for forty-nine years, during which time he served on the Fink Royal Commission into Technical Education and chaired the University's Finance Committee after the crisis of 1904. He became Vice-Chancellor in 1910, succeeding Sir John Madden as Chancellor in 1918 and retaining the position till his death. He died on the same day as the distinguished Master of another College, Dr E.H. Sugden of Queen's.

MacFarland's tenure was not all smooth sailing and the professors in particular chafed against the control which Council continued to exert over academic and financial matters, but MacFarland's skill as a committee chairman, personal charm and universally recognised integrity kept open revolt at bay. His standing in the community was such that he was asked to chair the 1931 meeting at which the Australian Citizens' League was founded.

MacFarland donated considerable sums of money during his lifetime, notably for scholarships at Ormond. The College was also to benefit from his estate. On his death, the University Council noted that 'Few men in any community, and almost no man in this community, can have won such universal esteem.'

Ella Annie Noble Macknight (1904–97)

Ella Macknight was a pioneer in several fields. When she graduated from the University of Melbourne in 1928, she was one of only five women in her year.

During her University years, she represented both Janet Clarke Hall and the University in hockey and golf. The latter was a lifelong interest and she was an active member of the Royal Melbourne Golf Club. Macknight was the first woman to receive a pilot's licence in Victoria. In 1930, she formed part of a six-woman escort for Amy Johnson when she landed in Melbourne after her solo flight from England. The team met Johnson in Laverton and flew to Moonee Valley, performing a tricky landing on the racecourse for the official reception before returning to Essendon.

Macknight's medical achievements were remarkable in many areas. Her long association with the Queen Victoria Hospital began in 1935. She was directly responsible for establishing the Oncology Department, which she headed for a decade, and she served as president of the hospital's board for six years in the 1970s. She spent nearly forty years on the Committee of the Victorian Red Cross and served on the Victorian Gynaecological Cytology Service and the Victorian Anti-Cancer Council. During World War II, she recalled working 'a twelve-hour day during the week with frequent night calls and weekend calls' for the Red Cross Blood Bank.

Macknight was Foundation Clinical Dean of the Monash Medical School at the Queen Victoria Hospital and the first woman President of the Australian Council of the Royal College of Obstetricians and Gynaecologists. She was instrumental in the formation of the Australian College of Obstetricians and Gynaecologists and the first Australian representative of the Asian Federation of Obstetrics and Gynaecology.

Ella Macknight's kinswoman, Elizabeth Chalmers Macknight (1977– , PhD 2003), teaches history at the University of Aberdeen. Her *Aristocratic Families in Republican France, 1870–1940* was published in 2012.

ॐ

Ethel Irene McLennan (1891–1983)

Ethel McLennan was one of seven women to graduate in the first generation of Biological Sciences students who attained the rank of lecturer or above under Baldwin Spencer. She was one of five to be awarded the DSc.

Her interest in botany began at Tintern Ladies' College, where she was taught by Georgina Sweet. A brilliant student, she graduated BSc with honours in 1914 and was appointed lecturer the following year. She was the first to teach mycology and plant pathology. She gained her DSc in 1921, and won the 1927 David Syme research prize for work on the endophytic fungus related to the seed of the grass Lolium. McLennan was appointed Associate Professor in 1931 and apart from a brief period as Acting Head of Department remained in this position until her retirement in 1957. Her expertise in the field of plant disease was widely appreciated and she travelled the country in the course of numerous consultancies. During World War II, she was one of the Melbourne University group working on making optical instruments to be used in the tropics proof against fungal infection.

'Dr Mac' was an influential figure in organisations supporting women in science in Australia. Within the University, she was active in Staff and Distaff and the Women of the University Fund. She occupied positions of national and international importance in the Victorian Women Graduates' Association, as President of the Australian Federation of University Women in 1934 and the Australian Pan-Pacific Women's Committee in 1929. She was a member of the Garden Committee at Como House and the Lyceum Club. McLennan is remembered particularly for her support of colleagues and students, support which was practical as well as moral.

In October 2000 Dr Sophie Ducker presented to the University the 103-year-old academic gown bequeathed to her by Dr Mac, who had herself inherited it from the first Professor of Botany and Plant Physiology, Alfred James Ewart.

Annie Jean Macnamara (1899–1968)

As a medical student graduating from the University of Melbourne in 1922, Jean Macnamara was part of an exceptional cohort which included Lucy Bryce, Macfarlane Burnet, Kate Campbell and Jean Littlejohn.

As resident and later clinical assistant (combined with a private practice) Macnamara specialised early in the treatment of poliomyelitis. The 1925 epidemic prompted her to test the use of immune serum in the treatment of pre-paralytic patients. In 1931 she published, with Macfarlane Burnet, their discovery of the existence of more than one strain of polio virus, work which contributed to the development of the Salk vaccine.

Following travel to America from 1931 to 1933 on a Rockefeller Fellowship, she devoted herself increasingly to conservative orthopaedics, often without charging a fee. In 1938 she established a clinic in Carlton, treating thirty children a day and providing a hot midday meal for them. As well as establishing country clinics, Macnamara served on numerous committees dealing with polio. Australia's first centre for disabled children was established at the Children's Hospital on her recommendation.

Macnamara's second career owed its inspiration to her love of the land. She was a pioneer in the use of myxomatosis to control rabbits. She had sent samples of the organism from America in 1933 only to have them dumped in Port Phillip Bay by Customs officials. Later tests from 1937 to 1944 in dry areas of the country failed to spread the disease, but a test along the Murray River in 1950 was more successful. In the 1952–53 season, myxomatosis was estimated to have augmented the Australian wool cheque by £30 million and the growers presented Macnamara with £800 and a clock. She was awarded an honorary LLD from the University of Melbourne in 1966.

Jean Macnamara continued to treat patients until her death from heart disease in 1968.

Phillip Henry Marcham (1830–1915)

'Good Old Marcham', as he was constantly called in its publications, served the University of Melbourne for over thirty years from 1881 until his death at the age of 85. Surprisingly, University publications such as *Alma Mater* and the *Melbourne Graduate*, while writing affectionately if patronisingly about him, frequently misspelt his actual names.

Marcham had worked as a university porter in England before migrating to Australia with his wife Margaret (1828?–1911), whom he married in 1856. They had six children—two daughters and four sons—but, unlike many other 'University servants' of the period, lived, not in a University cottage, but just outside the grounds in Leicester Street.

Marcham's job was that of porter and bell-ringer, the latter involving wielding a heavy hand-bell to signal the end of one class and the beginning of the next. In 1898, when he was sixty-eight years old, *Alma Mater* reported an incident that sheds light on some of his other duties and their perils:

> One day during a heavy gale, one of the windows above the staircase in the Union Rooms blew open, and Marcham climbed up to shut it and mend the catch which had broken. He had barely got it shut when a gust blew it violently open again. We may safely say that if it had not been for his fondness for sticking to the post of duty, he would have been thrown down, not merely to the foot of the ladder, but right to the foot of the stairs.

By 1912 the work was getting too much for him, but, since he pointed out that he had (not unexpectedly, given the size of his family) been unable to save enough to live on, the University offered him some 'light duties' on half pay. His unmarried daughter, Charlotte, perhaps sensibly, refused the offer of a cleaning job at a very low rate of pay.

Although many tributes, and a present to celebrate his fiftieth wedding anniversary, had been paid to Phillip Marcham, his death was barely noted by the Council, probably because with the whole University mourning the ongoing slaughter of its young men in the War, the passing of an elderly 'servant' seemed insignificant.

Marginson Family

Left to right: *David, Betty, Ray and Simon Marginson*

Raymond David Marginson (1923–) returned to the University from a career in the Commonwealth Public Service. As Vice-Principal from 1966 to 1988 he oversaw a restructure and modernisation of University administration and finances. His influence was felt in every aspect of the University, notably in the founding of the University Gallery and the site Master Plan. The award-winning underground carpark dates from this period. He was also part-time Chairman of Melbourne Water (1982–92) and President of Museum Victoria (1988–94).

Like Ray, Betty Marginson (1923–) was also active in student politics in the 1940s. After a career in primary school teaching she completed a postgraduate Diploma in Public Policy in 1985. Her lifelong interest in community affairs is evident in positions as President of University College from 1986 to 1991, office-bearer in a series of government-appointed bodies dealing with adult education and Chairman of the Victorian network of the University of the Third Age. She was the first woman Mayor of Hawthorn and was involved in the establishment of the Friends of the Baillieu Library.

The Marginsons' elder son Simon (1951–) was prominent in student affairs during the 1970s and *Farrago* editor in 1973. His PhD thesis 'Markets in education' won the Chancellor's Prize in 1997. He has been Professor of Higher Education in the Centre for the Study of Higher Education. He won the 2008 Woodward Medal in Humanities and Social Sciences for research from 2003 to 2007 into higher education and globalisation. His brother David (1955–) completed an outstanding MBA in 1988 and is now director of a national company.

Max Marginson (1928–2002) followed his brother Ray to the University, teaching and researching in biochemistry. He was a foundation member of the Australian Biochemical Society and taught students in several faculties, including Medicine, Agricultural Science and Science. He was a foundation member of University House and was three times Vice-President, four times President, and convenor of the wine-tasting panel for over fifteen years.

෴

George William Louis Marshall-Hall (1862–1915)

George Marshall-Hall ranks high on any list of University of Melbourne professors who have attracted controversy.

When he arrived in Melbourne in 1891 to take up the newly endowed Ormond Chair of Music, Marshall-Hall had already composed several operas, published articles in English music journals and worked as an organist and choirmaster. The year after his arrival, he founded the Marshall-Hall Orchestra, meeting its expenses himself until 1902 as well as paying the rent for the Melbourne University Conservatorium until 1905. The Marshall-Hall Orchestra was generally recognised to be as good as many European orchestras, and in 1908 funding was taken over by the Permanent Orchestra Trust Fund, under the patronage of Lady Northcote.

The socialist and atheist Marshall-Hall soon became friendly with the Heidelberg artists: not perhaps what turn-of-the-century Melbourne expected of a professor. In 1898 he was attacked by the *Argus*, which accused him of immorality and anti-clericalism, and suggested that women students, in particular, were not safe with him. Petitions and demonstrations followed, with Dr Leeper of Trinity College leading the charge against him and Lionel and Norman Lindsay mounting a spirited defence in the journal *Outpost*. In 1900 he lost his appointment but, since he was the lessee of the Conservatorium, he continued to teach. The University set up a rival teaching program. The Marshall-Hall Orchestra became unfinancial, however, and last performed in 1912.

The Ormond Chair of Music again fell vacant in 1914 and, despite controversy, Marshall-Hall was again offered the position in January 1915. In July of the same year, however, he died suddenly of appendicitis. His manuscripts were acquired by Percy Grainger for his Museum. His compositions, which were nearly all performed during his lifetime, have been revived by Richard Divall and recorded by the ABC. His influence on his contemporaries, musically and in relation to issues of free thought and free speech, was considerable.

Masson Family

David Orme Masson (1858–1937) came to the University of Melbourne in 1886 after a year as the first research assistant to the newly appointed professor of chemistry, William Ramsay, at Bristol University College: his son Irvine was to be Ramsay's last assistant in this post.

Orme Masson's migration to Australia with his bride Mary signalled a permanent commitment to this country and he refused several offers of prestigious appointments overseas to remain here. He was a gifted and charismatic lecturer, recalled by Kingsley Norris as 'the prince of demonstrators' and by Macfarlane Burnet as entrancing him with 'the wonder and glory of discovery'. Masson is perhaps less well-known for his own research, on topics including nitroglycerine, the velocity of migration of ions in solutions and the physical properties of liquids of the same chemical type, than for his abilities as an administrator. He was instrumental in the establishment of almost every significant scientific body of the twentieth century in Australia: the Society of Chemical Industry, the Council for Scientific and Industrial Research and the Royal Australian Chemical Institute. He was also involved for twenty-five years in Australia's Antarctic research program and chaired the Professorial Board from 1912 to 1926.

Mary Masson (1862–1945) was endowed with the same organisational skills as her husband. She was active in the Victoria League, the New Settlers' League, the Country Women's Association of Victoria, the Women of the University Fund and the University Branch of the Australian Red Cross Society. She regularly attended meetings of the University Chemical Society.

The Massons had three children, one of whom predeceased them: Elsie Rosaline (1891–1935), wife of the anthropologist Bronislaw Malinowski, and the author of *An Untamed Territory: The Northern Territory of Australia* (1915). James Irvine (1887–1962) gained renown as a historian of chemistry and bibliographer. Flora Marjorie (Marnie) Bassett (1889–1980) was a foundation member of the Australian Academy of the Humanities and author of several works, the best-known of which is *The Hentys: An Australian Colonial Tapestry* (1954). *The Lady Masso Lectures: 1949–2001*, edited by Valda M. McRae, was published in 2003 and *Finding Home: The Masson Family*, by Richard Selleck, was published in 2013.

☙❧

Ernst Artur Franz Joseph Matthaei (1904–66)

Ernst Matthaei migrated to Australia from Germany in 1929 as the agent for Zeiss optical instruments, working initially for the firm of E.C. Heyne & Co. He had graduated Diplom-optiker from the University of Jena. In the 1930s he established his own firm, dealing in scientific instruments. He married Grace Moran Villiers in May 1939 and was naturalised the following month. Grace Matthaei (1910–82, BA DipEd) was a journalist who worked in the Geology Library of the University from 1953 to 1978. She was largely responsible for the exchange arrangements with overseas institutions, which laid foundations of a journal collection of national importance.

The outbreak of war devastated Ernst Matthaei's business, since imports from Germany ceased, and Matthaei accepted R.D. ('Pansy') Wright's offer of a junior position in the Department of Physiology. Two years later he began a significant contribution to the war effort when he was transferred to the Botany Department and put in charge of the annexe which made graticules for sighting telescopes and binoculars. Matthaei was part of the team which successfully solved the problem of making optical instruments proof against multi-fungal infections.

In 1945 Matthaei proposed that the annexe and its team, which he had turned into a well-staffed service laboratory and workshop, become the service centre for the University's opto-mechanical equipment. In 1949 he gave a series of lecture-demonstrations for researchers on the optical microscope which was so popular it was repeated and offered in later years to final-year Science students.

Ernst Matthaei was a foundation member of University House and the Ernst Matthaei Memorial Collection of Early Glass, which commemorates his lifelong interest in glass, is on display in the Lower East dining room, renamed the Matthaei Room in his honour in 2000. Additions are still made to this collection through the fund established by his friends.

✑

Ian Ramsay Maxwell (1901–79)

Ian Maxwell's literary bent declared itself early: he published poems in and became editor of the *Scotch Collegian*. Although he published little poetry in later life, his 'Vespers' was chosen as the first in H.M. Green's 1946 anthology *Modern Australian Poetry*. He had, however, on graduation from the University of Melbourne (BA 1923, LLB 1925), begun professional life as a barrister, practising until he left for further study at Balliol College. In 1934–36 he taught English at the University of Copenhagen. He took his BLitt from Oxford in 1935.

Beatrice Muriel Maxwell (1901–99), whom he married in 1926, was a distinguished scholar in her own right. She tutored in the English Department and was a much-loved and respected teacher in several Melbourne schools, including Ruyton Girls' School, where she taught from 1960 to 1972. Muriel Maxwell, who was the daughter of R.J.A. Berry, Professor of Anatomy at the University, took her BA in 1922 and her MA in 1972.

In 1936 Ian Maxwell began a decade in the English Department at Sydney University, during which, Chris Wallace-Crabbe tells us, he grew tomatoes on the top of the tower of the Great Quad while acting as air-raid precautions officer. In 1946 he returned to Melbourne, taking the Chair of English Language and Literature, which he occupied until 1968. He was Dean of Arts from 1948 to 1950, and, with 'Pansy' Wright, one of the leading opponents of the Commonwealth Government's 1950 attempt to ban the Communist Party of Australia.

Maxwell was an inspirational lecturer, reciting Milton, Norse sagas and Robert Burns with passion and the occasional tear. His interests were broad, from Old Icelandic literature, the Border ballads and French romances to Yeats, Eliot, E.M. Forster and Aldous Huxley. He remained a familiar figure on campus until his death, although only spending, as Wallace-Crabbe tells us, 'six and a half days at the University instead of seven'.

John Dudley Gibbs Medley (1891–1962)

John Medley, succeeding Raymond Priestley in 1938 as Vice-Chancellor, was elected by the narrowest of margins, a single vote separating him from Professor Douglas Copland. Despite his establishment background and Oxford degree, he might have seemed an odd choice for the position, having, after service in Flanders during World War I, worked in the family business of Antony Gibbs & Sons and its Australian branch, Gibbs, Bright & Co., before taking over as Headmaster of Tudor House, a preparatory school at Moss Vale, NSW.

In fact, he surprised his supporters as much as his opponents, demonstrating, despite his membership of exclusive clubs and acquaintance with the political and social elite, a considerable radicalism in his conduct of University business. Within a short time of his appointment, the long-running dispute between the professors and council over who should exercise executive control was resolved. The Chancellor, Sir James Barrett, had been replaced, and authority had shifted decisively to the professors. By the time he resigned in 1951, the University had been transformed.

Medley chaired the Vice-Chancellors' Committee for ten years and one of his greatest achievements came late in his career—negotiating the agreement of the newly elected Prime Minister Robert Menzies to academic salary increases, which saved other universities from decline after the establishment of the ANU, which was then offering superior pay and conditions.

Medley was active and well-known in all aspects of Australian cultural life—on the Board of the ABC, the National Gallery and the Public Library—and his 500 weekly pieces on the front page of the *Age Literary Supplement* brought him an army of admirers for his civilised and tolerant views, his defence of free speech and correct English, and his occasional forays into verse. He is probably not the only Vice-Chancellor who felt as he did at six o'clock, but he is probably the only one to have expressed his feelings so cogently:

I thank Thee, Lord, for every Prof.
Who lives a very long way off.
They're sneaking homeward, one by one:
Now we can get some business done!
Just think (how horrible it sounds)
If everyone lived in the Grounds!

Robert Gordon Menzies (1894–1978)

Front row from left: *Robert Menzies, Dame Pattie Menzies and Pandit Nehru*

Summarising the career of Australia's longest-serving Prime Minister is no easy task. The life of Robert Menzies spanned a time when he could announce, without fear of controversy, that because Britain had declared war on Germany, Australia was also at war, through his proclamation that he was 'British to his bootstraps', and a declaration of undying love to a young Queen, to a time when mass rallies began demanding an Australian republic.

Menzies was born in Jeparit, educated in Ballarat, and, with the aid of scholarships, at Wesley College. His career at the University of Melbourne (LLB 1916, LLM 1918) was brilliant, combining academic success with prominence in student affairs. From 1928 to 1934 he served in both Houses of the Victorian Parliament, while simultaneously maintaining a successful legal practice. In 1934 he won the Federal seat of Kooyong, an electorate he represented until his retirement from politics. Having served briefly as Prime Minister from 1939 to 1941, he was re-elected in 1949 and remained in office until 1966.

The Liberal/Country Party coalition which he was at pains to establish and preserve endures to this day. Menzies was unsuccessful in his attempt to have the Communist Party banned in 1951 but extremely successful in exploiting fears of communism, notably after the defection of Vladimir Petrov in 1954. The 'Menzies years' saw Australian society transformed, as a long economic boom and accelerated migration from Europe changed its composition and physical environment.

Menzies was responsible for an expansion of Federal government funding of education. Implementation of the recommendations Sir Keith Murray's 1956 inquiry into Australian universities provided desperately needed funding while preserving their autonomy. The Colombo Plan brought students from the Third World to Australian universities. Provision of funding in 1960 for the construction of Lake Burley Griffin transformed the national capital and the establishment of the ANU provided new opportunities for research.

He was Chancellor of the University 1967–72 and part of his personal library was presented to the Baillieu Library in 1978.

☙

The Millis Sisters

Jean Jackson's death in March followed by that of her younger sister Nancy Millis in September 2012 brought to an end a remarkable association with the University of two scientists of distinction that had extended over more than seventy years. Both of Frank and Annie Millis's two daughters went from scholarships at private secondary schools to long careers in biochemistry, although they approached the discipline from very different angles.

Jean Millis Jackson (1913–2012), who took her BSc in 1934, with the Exhibition in Biochemistry, made her most distinguished contribution in the sometimes neglected field of dietetics and nutrition. Her initial research output was slow in coming, principally because of the extraordinary teaching load involved in giving classes in biochemistry to students in Science, Medicine and Dentistry, but she

Jean Millis Jackson

made up for this when, in 1950, she left for the University of Malaya in Singapore, from which she took her PhD in 1954. She published ten research papers between 1954 and 1958. Before that, she had been able to indulge what became a lifelong passion for ship travel, by travelling to Cambridge in 1944 to take up a British Council Scholarship: her journey on a cargo trip via the Panama Canal and across the Atlantic in a convoy took eight weeks.

In 1957 Jean Millis married Arthur Jackson, who was to become the Chief Scientist of Singapore. They returned to Melbourne in 1960 where she returned briefly to the Department of Biochemistry, resigning in 1964. She was a consultant to the World Health Organization Applied Nutrition Program and the World Bank's nutrition work in Indonesia. She was instrumental in the establishment of the Dietetics Association of Victoria and a very active member of the Victorian Women Graduates Association: the Jean Jackson Bursary was established in her honour.

Unlike her sister, Nancy Fannie Millis (1922–2012) did not go straight from school to University: her father's severe illness made it necessary for her to find paid work and study part-time. Debarred from entering the Science course because she had taken the matriculation examination over two years, she entered the Faculty of Agriculture and from the moment she pulled on her gumboots became a devoted 'Aggie'.

Millis's initial work in New Guinea in 1948 almost led to her death and she was saved only by streptomycin, which had just become available. The following year, she won a scholarship to Bristol University, where she researched spoilage in cider, returning in 1945

Nancy Millis

with her PhD and a skill that was to stand her in good stead as judge of cider in numerous Agricultural Shows. She joined the Department of Microbiology in 1953. Later work in America and Japan led to her co-authorship of *Biochemical Engineering*, which became a standard textbook, translated into Czech, Polish and Spanish.

In 1982, Nancy Millis became the fourth woman to be appointed to a chair at Melbourne University. She undertook research in genetic engineering and later in water quality. Millis served as Chancellor of La Trobe University from 1992 to 2006, maintaining an active research profile and a presence on the Melbourne campus throughout. She took particular interest in the development of higher education courses and links between universities and industry, and chaired the Genetic Manipulation Advisory Committee. Among her many awards and honorary degrees, she received an Australia Post Legends Award in 2002, a Centenary Medal in 2003 and the ATSE Clunies Ross Award for the application of science and technology for the economic, social or environmental benefit of Australia in 2007.

John Monash (1865–1931)

Geoffrey Serle describes John Monash, in the *Australian Dictionary of Biography*, as 'one tall poppy who was never cut down' despite the fact that he was overtly ambitious, status-conscious and sensitive to slights. His career was to have considerable variety, despite his certainty from an early age that he would be an engineer.

His University career did not run smoothly: the competing demands of the general cultural life of Melbourne and student affairs were too compelling. He was a co-founder of the Melbourne University Union and editor of the first dozen issues of *Melbourne University Review*.

While still a part-time student, he was put in charge of the construction of the Outer Circle railway line and, in 1890, took up a position with the Melbourne Harbor Trust. He graduated MEng in 1893, BA, LLB in 1895. The following year he sat the examinations for Major, having joined the Metropolitan Brigade of the Garrison Artillery in 1887. By 1896, he had taken ninety-four written examinations in seventeen years.

Monash combined his military career with managing his private engineering company, Reinforced Concrete and Monier Pipe Construction Co. Ltd, and lecturing in Engineering at the University, where he was also Chairman of the Graduates' Association and President of the University Club.

He sailed with the AIF at the end of 1914 and proved an outstanding general during the campaigns at Gallipoli and in France. His achievement of the repatriation of 160,000 Australian soldiers, accomplished almost entirely in eight months, was no less remarkable.

In 1920, Monash became General Manager of the State Electricity Commission of Victoria. Within ten years the grid, powered by Gippsland brown coal, covered the state.

Monash was Vice-Chancellor of the University from 1923 until his death. He led Melbourne's Anzac Day march from 1925 and was President of the Australasian Association for the Advancement of Science in 1924–26. Although he had not always maintained close links with the Jewish community, he became a member of the Board of Management of the St Kilda Congregation and National President of the Australian Zionist Federation in 1927.

જી

Charles Edmund Moorhouse (1911–2002)

Charles Moorhouse with 'Pansy' Wright

Charles Moorhouse was foundation President of University House and the driving force behind its establishment. His commitment to collegiality and friendships across disciplines was evident throughout his thirty-year association with the University.

Both his parents were Melbourne graduates. William Moorhouse graduated MA in 1909 and Ruth Elinor Topp, among the University's first women graduates, took her MA the following year. In 1917 Ruth died and the Moorhouse children were raised by their maternal grandparents.

Moorhouse graduated in Mechanical Engineering in 1933 and Electrical Engineering the following year. He spent 1933–36 as Demonstrator and Senior Demonstrator in Engineering, working in England from 1936–38, and with the then State Electricity Commission of Victoria until 1945. He was seconded to the Royal Australian Engineers in 1940 and the Munitions Supply Laboratories at Maribyrnong in 1941–42.

In 1946 Engineering was divided into separate Departments of Mechanical, Civil and Electrical Engineering and Moorhouse rejoined the staff as the first Lecturer-in-Charge of Electrical Engineering. He was appointed to a Chair within two years.

The 1950s saw enormous changes in courses and subjects. Moorhouse, a lover of languages, literature and art, introduced painting and philosophy in the Engineering curriculum as well as incorporating teacher training for lecturers in his Department.

He was a prolific writer on subjects ranging from the history of Melbourne Grammar School and the Engineering School at Melbourne University to power sources, links and loads. He edited *Visual Messages* (1979, 1986). One of his most popular articles was 'Engineering and Cookery', published in *Cranks and Nuts*.

He was twice Dean of Engineering, a member of the Council of University Women's College, chair of the Victorian Universities and Schools Examination Board, a member of the Melbourne Grammar School Council for twenty-one years and of the Interim Council of the Royal Military College Duntroon for a decade.

Moshinsky Family

In 1952 the seventeen-year-old Samson Moshinsky hitch-hiked to Sydney from Melbourne to greet his parents and two younger brothers on their arrival in Australia from Shanghai. The family had come almost to the end of a protracted journey which had begun in 1921 when they had travelled from Vladivostok and Southern Russia to Harbin and Shanghai, fleeing the Russian Revolution. Sam arrived in Australia unaccompanied in 1951, found accommodation for the family in Melbourne and went back to Sydney to meet them the following year.

Left to right: *Sam, Eva, Elijah, Nathan and Abraham, c. 1952*

All three of the Moshinskys' sons took degrees at the University of Melbourne. Sam Moshinsky (1934–) took his BCom in 1959. In 2000 he was awarded an OAM for services to the Jewish community, particularly through charitable religious and cultural activities. His wife, Ada Moshinsky (1940–), graduated LLB in 1964 and LLM in 1977. Their son, Mark Moshinsky SC (1965–) took his BA in 1988 and LLB in 1989, co-editing that year's *Melbourne University Law Review*. He is a Senior Fellow (Melbourne Law Masters).

Nathan Moshinsky QC (1941–) took his LLB in 1963 and BA in 1967. His areas of practice included trade practices and administrative law, and he served as Solicitor-General of the Solomon Islands from 2003 to 2006. He is also an accomplished painter who describes his work as an exploration of the relationship between the physical world and that of the imagination. His wife, Anne Moshinsky (1941–), graduated BA in 1964 and BLitt in 1982. Their daughter, Natasha Moshinsky (1972–), took her BA in 1996 and BSocW in 2000.

The third son, Elijah Moshinsky (1946–), made a considerable impression in student theatre during his time as an undergraduate. He took his BA from Melbourne University in 1968, and PhD from Oxford. He is known to opera and theatre audiences world-wide as a director. The first opera he directed was *Peter Grimes*, a production which was filmed in 1981. Moshinsky has directed a dozen operas for Opera Australia. His theatre productions include five of the BBC Shakespeare cycle and West End productions including *Cyrano de Bergerac*. TV watchers will recall a program on his production of *The Abduction from the Seraglio*, staged in the Topkapi Palace in Istanbul. He has directed many works at Royal Opera House, Covent Garden, and his acclaimed *Simon Boccanegra* was revived there under the baton of Sir Antonio Pappano in 2013.

Stephen Murray-Smith (1922–88)

At the celebration of Stephen Murray-Smith's life and work a fortnight after his death, Geoffrey Serle noted that 'His range and breadth were quite unusual in this country. Very few academics in modern times remotely rival his diverse interests and knowledge.'

As well as editing *Overland* for over thirty years, Murray-Smith edited *Melbourne Studies in Education* for twelve and published on subjects as diverse as the islander communities of Bass Strait, the history of technical education in Victoria and Antarctic research. He edited the *Dictionary of Australian Quotations* (1984) and wrote *Right Words: A Guide to English Usage in Australia* (1987). He was also a quiz champion, working with Barry Jones, Zelman Cowen, Rohan Rivett and others on programs including 3DB's *Information Please* and *Beat the Brains* on the ABC.

Murray-Smith came relatively late to academia. He served with the AIF in New Guinea from 1942 to 1945 and worked in Prague for the Telepress news agency. In 1966, having completed a PhD on technical education, he joined the Melbourne University Department of Education, where he worked from 1966 to 1987. His colleague Gwyneth Dow affirmed, 'I have never known him to be unkind as a supervisor, editor or reviewer.'

Stephen Murray-Smith was a campaigner for many causes. A member of the Communist Party from student days, he resigned in 1956 and joined the ALP. He was an advocate of manned lighthouses and supported many environmental causes. He chaired the National Book Council from 1981 to 1983, having earlier fought in the Freedom to Read campaign against Victorian censorship of Mary McCarthy's *The Group* and *The Trial of Lady Chatterley's Lover*. He was prominent in the Victorian anti-hanging campaigns of the 1960s and served on the Advisory Council on Australian Archives and the Board of the Film and TV School.

Joanna Murray-Smith (1962– , BA 1986), daughter of Nita (BA 1973) and Stephen Murray-Smith, is one of Australia's most popular playwrights, whose work for stage and television, including *Love Child*, *Greed*, *Honour* and *Cassidy* has won many awards.

∾

Rose Mushin (1905–2002)

Rose Chapman was born in Poland and her early interest in science may have been stimulated by the admiration her headmistress showed for the work of a fellow Polish scientist, Marie Curie, who was a personal friend.

Her scientific studies at the universities of Krakow and later Warsaw were interrupted when she moved with her family to Australia in 1927. There she married Alick Mushin.

Despite the Depression and helping her husband in his work, Mushin resumed her studies, graduating BSc in 1938 and MSc in 1944. She worked in the Department of Bacteriology under Professor Sydney Rubbo and in 1950 was awarded a PhD for her thesis entitled 'Bacteriological Aspects of Gastroenteritis'. Her work on E. coli was groundbreaking, proving that certain strains produce gastroenteritis.

Mushin was notable in the Department not only for her high number of publications, but also for her dedication to teaching. She taught students in both Science and Agricultural Science. She was also welcomed as a visiting researcher overseas, attending both the Rockefeller and Pasteur Institutes.

When she retired in 1970, Mushin joined her daughters Adeerah and Elora in Israel, but was not left unemployed, being recruited instead by a local veterinary institute to help in the control of animal diseases. She worked there for another decade before retiring again to devote herself to voluntary work with the blind and the aged, and caring for her grandchildren.

Elora Mushin (1942–) is also a Melbourne alumna. She took her GradDipSocStuds in 1963 and BA the following year.

Edward John Nanson (1850–1936)

Staff complaining of cramped working conditions might be chastened by the account provided by E.J. Nanson of his accommodation for over ten years in the Old Quadrangle. He had a dining room, drawing room, two bedrooms, bathroom and kitchen for himself, his wife and the five children he had at the time. 'I have no study and am obliged to do all my work in my dining room,' he told Council, 'whereas every other Professor … has a study at the University.' In September 1885 he was finally accommodated in what is now University House.

Nanson was appointed to the Chair of Pure and Mixed Mathematics following the death of the Foundation Professor, W.P. Wilson. He arrived from England in 1875 and spent a record forty-eight years in his position. He was a notable theoretician, especially in matrix theory, regularly published in scholarly journals, and became foundation President of the Mathematics Association of Victoria.

Mathematics was not a popular subject and Nanson, frustrated by the cavalier attitude of Engineering and Arts students for whom it was compulsory, acquired a reputation as a stern disciplinarian. He was, however, a kindly, though reserved man and a notable field naturalist.

Nanson was a fervent proponent of parliamentary representation based on a preferential voting system, publishing and speaking widely on this subject. Despite support from Alfred Deakin and George Turner, preferential voting was not introduced until 1918.

He was a Trustee of the Public Library and National Gallery of Victoria from 1879 to 1913 and is commemorated by the University through the annual award of the Professor Nanson Prize.

Nanson had ten children. His daughter Joan worked almost continuously at the University from 1935 to 1974, so that their careers together span a century of its history. Joan Wettenhall Nanson (1913–2008) was Secretary to both Raymond Priestley and John Medley and subsequently to the Warden of the Mildura Branch of the University, before becoming Secretary to successive Deans of Graduate Studies.

❧

Nettie Palmer (1885–1964), Helen Palmer (1917–79)

Niece and great-niece respectively of Henry Bournes Higgins, Janet (Nettie) Palmer and her daughter Helen exerted an enduring influence on the cultural life of Australia.

Nettie Higgins took her BA in 1909 and after a year in Europe returned to take her MA in 1912. Her marriage in 1914 to Edward Vivian (Vance) Palmer established one of Australia's most significant literary partnerships. Herself the author of two collections of poems, literary criticism, local histories and a memoir of her uncle, Nettie also wrote *Fourteen Years: Extracts from a Private Journal, 1925–1939*, published in 1948, and pamphlets on the Spanish Civil War. She is perhaps best remembered for her literary contacts and the support and judicious critical appraisal she and Vance extended to new and established Australian writers. Her *Henry Handel Richardson* (1950) was the first full-length study of the author whom she had known for twenty-five years. Her critical work appeared mostly in newspapers and journals. It exposed many Australian writers such as Martin Boyd, Barbara Baynton and Frank Dalby Davison to their first serious critical attention.

Nettie Palmer

Nettie Palmer's work was the subject of a special issue of *Meanjin* in 1959 and is examined in Drusilla Modjeska's *Exiles at Home* (1981). In 1999, Deborah Jordan published *Nettie Palmer: Search for an Aesthetic*.

Helen Palmer was honoured after her death by a memorial publication, *Helen Palmer's Outlook* (1982). A member of the Communist Party of Australia until 1957, Helen graduated in Arts and Education from the University of Melbourne, and after wartime service, during which she was in charge of educational services provided by WAAAF personnel throughout Australia, she became a secondary school teacher. Helen published numerous textbooks for high schools, but her most significant contribution to Australian culture lay in the journal she founded and edited: *Outlook: An Australian Socialist Review.*

☙

Maria Annunziata Gröbner Pietzcker (1897–1983)

When Maria Pietzcker died the bequest of her property in Research to the Howard Florey Institute was the culmination of thirty years of giving, amounting, in labour and money, to several hundred thousand dollars in value.

Maria Gröbner, the daughter of an Austrian doctor, came to Melbourne in the 1920s after the dissolution of a short-lived marriage. She made an immediate impact as a sophisticated woman of culture and, above all, if one is to judge from the contemporary press, of fashion. She returned to Europe several times, and the Australian newspapers reported her views on clothes as seriously as her assessment of the political situation.

In 1953 she married the retired former Swiss Consul, John Alexander Pietzcker (1870–1958), a very popular Consul for almost two decades. As well as providing assistance to Italians in Australia during World War II, he endowed an annual chess tournament and held lavish Swiss National Day parties at his Toorak house. On his death he too remembered the University, leaving a bequest of £20,000 for 'the furtherance and encouragement of the study of Mental Hygiene'.

On his death, Madame Pietzcker began an extraordinary association with the University. She initially volunteered her services to 'Pansy' Wright, organising and operating the glassware service for the new steroid chromatography section of the Ionic Research Unit. This was high-precision work, requiring great skill, and she soon took on other organisational tasks, eventually proving an exceptional surgical assistant. She continued this work, in an entirely voluntary capacity, for twenty years and, after each of her frequent trips to Europe, she presented much-needed equipment to the Florey. The Madame Pietzcker Surgical Suite was named in recognition of her generosity.

The property at Research supported another of Madame Pietzcker's interests: 'Cold Comfort Farm' was a herb nursery from which she supplied the garden trade.

Surprisingly, the only image of Maria Pietzcker to be found is the medallion by Michael Meszaros commissioned by the Florey and displayed in University House.

கூ

Muriel Jean Polglaze (1911–78)

When Jean Polglaze (BCom 1931) took her Masters in Economics in 1936, she was the first woman in Australia to do so and, when she was appointed in the Faculty of Economics in 1939, she was its sole female lecturer. Despite her undoubted brilliance (she had taken honours in eleven of the fifteen subjects in her undergraduate degree and won a Rockefeller Foundation fellowship to study at Cambridge University) the *Sydney Morning Herald* story about her was headed 'Golden-Haired Economist' and began its account by stressing that she was 'a slim graceful girl, obviously in her early twenties, with lovely red gold hair, and a very modest, but most attractive personality'.

She spent her Fellowship years studying the measurement and analysis of investment and in 1940, at the invitation of Prime Minister Robert Menzies, established the Statistical Section of the Department of Defence Co-ordination, which collated and analysed statistics supplied by the Departments of Navy, Army and Air, and Munitions and Aircraft Production. She was to continue to work there part-time throughout the war, simultaneously continuing to teach, including delivering lectures in Statistical Method twice a week at 8.00 a.m., repeating them in the evenings.

It is in fact as a teacher and Faculty administrator that Polglaze is best remembered by many academic economists, including the late Peter Karmel. Despite enrolments in her courses of several hundred students every year, Polglaze maintained a close watch over individual students, advising candidates for the newly established honours degree on research topics for their theses. Jean Polglaze served as Sub-Dean of the Faculty for many years and wrote the article on the Consumer Price Index for *The Australian Encyclopedia* published in 1984.

The four Jean Polglaze Memorial Prizes for undergraduate students were established in 1980 in her memory.

Preston Family

William Preston

Three generations of the Preston family lived in the University grounds from the end of the nineteenth century to well into the twentieth.

William Henry Voils Preston (1868–1941) virtually embodied the Anatomy Department for many staff and students. Like so many technical staff, he possessed a wide variety of skills: in England he had been a theatre dresser and a fully qualified masseur. He was also a very skilled photographer. He came to the University from the Melbourne Hospital in 1896. K.F. Russell tells us that 'he was a kindly, helpful person with a very keen sense of humour, a fund of good stories and a lively appreciation of good whiskey ... His great hobby was campanology'. Always addressed as Mr Preston, he was intensely loyal to the Medical School, with an extraordinary knowledge of its staff and students.

His duties were both onerous and varied, including receiving cadavers, embalming and ordering all supplies. Russell also details the unorthodox assistance he was known to give to candidates at the operative surgery examination for the MS. When he died in 1941, after forty-five years' service, and his funeral procession moved along Swanston Street to the Melbourne General Cemetery, the bell ringers of St Paul's Cathedral, where he had rung the bells, honoured his passing with a muffled peal.

William Preston was succeeded in his position by his son Leonard Joseph Kent Preston (1904–87). Having joined the Department in 1932 at the age of twenty-eight, Leonard Preston succeeded his father in 1942 and retired after thirty-eight years' service at the beginning of 1970. The Council Minute on his retirement records that, having been born in the University grounds, he had seen the Medical School transformed:

> He was born in the original medical school building of 1862—he grew up alongside the new medical school of 1885—he served in the Anatomy building opened in 1923 and he worked in the tri-radiate building occupied in 1968, a record of long association which will almost certainly never be matched.

One of William Preston's children, who grew up in the house in the grounds, Sidney Gordon Preston (1909–88) took his MB BS in 1938, continuing, although he did not work in a Department, this long family association with the University.

☙

Raymond Edward Priestley (1886–1974)

Sir Mark Oliphant remarked that as Vice-Chancellor of the University of Melbourne, Raymond Priestley saw himself as the 'manager of a large business', whereas as Principal and Vice-Chancellor of the University of Birmingham from 1938, he saw his position as that of 'spokesman for the academic staff and the students'. His career at Melbourne reflected this tension while demonstrating his aptitude for both aspects of the position.

Northern Party of Scott's 2nd Expedition
From left: *Raymond E. Priestley, Victor L.A. Campbell and George P. Abbott*

Priestley was recruited to join Shackleton's 1907–09 expedition to Antarctica as a geologist while in his final year of science at University College, Bristol, and his scientific work with Edgeworth David earned him a position on Scott's second expedition of 1910–13. Priestley formed part of the group trapped (in summer outfits) at Terra Nova Bay which survived the winter by digging a snow cave and eating seal and penguin meat. His war service won him the Military Cross and in 1919 he was seconded to the War Office to write the history of the signal service. He graduated BA in 1920, DipAg in 1922 from Christ's College, Cambridge, and was elected fellow of Clare College the same year. In 1924 he began his career in university administration at Cambridge, filling three positions simultaneously.

Priestley accepted appointment as the University of Melbourne's first salaried Vice-Chancellor in 1934. He worked energetically for scholarships, additional staff, a new library and research facilities. His greatest success was perhaps the opening of the students' Union House. The battle for executive control of the University between the Vice-Chancellor and the Chancellor, Sir James Barrett, was not resolved during Priestley's tenure and, despite receiving Council support, Priestley resigned in 1938. He returned to England the same year as Vice-Chancellor and Principal of the University of Birmingham. After retirement he held senior positions in numerous scientific and policy organisations and revisited Antarctica in 1956 and 1959.

Both in England and Australia Priestley made his mark as a man of science, a humane and able administrator and tireless advocate of the importance of the University in the wider community. *The Diary of a Vice-Chancellor: University of Melbourne, 1935–1938*, edited by Ronald Ridley, was published in 2002.

જી

Sydney Dattilo Rubbo (1911–69)

Sydney Rubbo was born in Sydney and took his first degrees (BSc, 1934; DipBact, 1935; PhD, 1937) in Sydney and London before joining the University of Melbourne department he was to transform over two and a half decades. He was awarded an MD from Melbourne in 1955 and a DSc from London in 1966. Rubbo joined the Department of Bacteriology in 1938, and in the following year took the unusual step of undertaking studies in Medicine side by side with students to whom he lectured. He graduated MB BS in 1943, returning to the Department in 1944 on completion of his residency, and succeeded Harold Woodruff as Professor in 1945.

After his doctoral studies on *Penicillium roqueforti*, Rubbo's first interest was in chemotherapy, and his work with Adrien Albert led to the production of the antiseptic aminacrine, said to be the first Australian drug recognised by the *British Pharmacopoeia*. During the war, Rubbo worked on the prevention of typhoid, and later on therapies against tuberculosis. His work in prevention of infection ranged from reducing cross-infection in hospitals to the sterilisation of a spacecraft to prevent importation of organisms from Earth to outer space. The Department (renamed Microbiology in 1964) was finally accommodated in a new building in 1965.

Sydney Rubbo's interests extended well beyond the University. A campaigner against the Vietnam War and the use of chemical and biological agents in war, he was also President of the Dante Alighieri Society and took a considerable interest in the arts.

Many members of the University have long bought their books at the first Readings bookshop in Carlton, run since 1976 by Mark Rubbo, one of Rubbo's two sons. His elder son, Michael, is a well-known film director and painter. Anna Rubbo (BArch 1965) is Associate Professor at the University of Sydney and Kiffy Rubbo was an inspirational and influential Director of the Ewing Gallery at the University of Melbourne.

☙❧

Norman William Saffin (1916–2002)

In the obituary page of *The Age* Peter Beilharz paid tribute to a teacher who 'turned on the lights for droves of students who passed through his class'. In the state educational system, he was a man of exceptional academic distinction and breadth of attainment.

Norman Saffin was born in Terang, the son of a stationhand. During the Depression he left school to go rabbitting with his father and worked as a postman before becoming a student teacher in 1936. Two years later, he was Head Teacher of a country school. In 1939 he married Susan Ellen Williams (1926–91) and entered the Melbourne Teachers' College, paying his own fees.

Susan and Norman Saffin taught in Victorian country schools. After taking his BA and Diplomas in Commerce and Public Administration in 1951, Saffin took his MA from Melbourne University in 1954, with a thesis entitled 'French Positivism: Its Antecedents and Its Effects on the Practice of French Historiography', and the following year he and Susan travelled to England where he took his PhD from the University of London.

When Susan and Norman Saffin returned to Australia they taught at schools in Colac, Seymour and Ringwood before their final posting at Croydon High School, where Susan Saffin was the librarian and her husband taught history and literature. He also published two books: *Science, Religion and Education in Britain, 1804–1904* in 1973 and *Left and Right in Bendigo and Shepparton, 1947–51* the following year. His projected five-volume *History of the Victorian Workingman*, intended to cover the period from the Gold Rushes to the Labor Party Split of 1955, remains unpublished, but the manuscript may be consulted in the University Archives.

Saffin's scholarship was sustained by an extraordinary personal library of about 15,000 volumes covering the social sciences and humanities. His dedication to his pupils was evidenced by his teaching: he taught evening classes until his retirement.

❦

Richard Herbert Samuel (1900–83)

When Richard Samuel arrived in Melbourne to become Head of the Department of Germanic Studies in 1947, he had already had a distinguished career. He served in the German Army in 1918, graduated DrPhil. from the University of Berlin in 1923 and occupied a number of academic posts in Germany before fleeing the anti-Jewish purges in 1934.

He held various academic positions at Cambridge University and the London School of Economics until the outbreak of World War II. During a 1938 visit to Prague he facilitated the escape of the leader of the German Democratic Socialist Party in the Czech Parliament, Wenzel Jaksch, to England. In 1940, however, he was interned for almost six months as an 'enemy alien', and released only to join the British Army.

Samuel's Army work did not end with the outbreak of war: he was a Research Officer in the Political Intelligence Department of the Foreign Office from 1943–46. The Samuel family travelled to Australia on the same ship as Louis Matheson, who was joining the Department of Civil Engineering.

During his twenty years in the Department of Germanic Studies, Samuel oversaw the expansion of the Dutch program and the establishment of Swedish. He was the driving force behind the establishment of the Goethe Society in Victoria and his lectures on interwar Germany attracted much public interest.

Samuel's scholarship took two principal directions. He published influential studies of the German education system, notably *Education and Society in Modern Germany* (1949), and two editions of the works of Novalis. The second project was to occupy him from 1953 onwards, incorporating manuscripts discovered after the war.

Under Richard Samuel, German studies in Australia took a high profile at home and abroad. Samuel's professional library, including manuscripts, diaries and an exceptional collection of German textbooks, was acquired by the University Library after his death.

❧

Bartholomew Augustine Santamaria (1915–98)

Few men have had as significant an effect on Australian public life as Bob Santamaria. The Democratic Labor Party he was instrumental in founding helped keep the Liberal/ Country Party coalition in power for seventeen years, his influence over the trade union movement was profound and his print and electronic media pronouncements were both influential and controversial.

Santamaria (BA 1935, LLB 1936, MA 1959) was the son of Sicilian migrants who originally settled in Brunswick. At the University he joined the Campion Society in 1932 and became remarkable for his part in a 1937 debate in the Public Lecture Theatre on the Spanish Civil War, in which he spoke against the Republican government. Manning Clark later recalled his charismatic performance. Nettie Palmer was one of the anti-Franco speakers.

Santamaria founded the *Catholic Worker* in 1936 and later *News Weekly*. His regular television program, *Point of View*, later provided another avenue of communication. The Archbishop of Melbourne, Daniel Mannix, was a deep and permanent influence, appointing Santamaria to the secretariat of Catholic Action in 1937. He was Director of Catholic Action in 1947–54 and President of the Catholic Social Movement in 1943–57.

The Movement, renamed in 1957 the National Civic Council, was a dominant force in Australian politics, working openly and covertly against communist influence in the labour movement. The Democratic Labor Party, which the divisive actions of the NCC brought into being, ensured a conservative Federal government from 1955 to 1972. Victory in the key policy area of state support of Catholic and other independent schools, however, required a long battle.

Seven of Santamaria's eight children are graduates of Melbourne University. Among them, Mary Helen Woods (1942–) took her BMus in 1964 and is Vice-President of the Australian Family Movement, and Catherine (1943–2012) took her BA in 1968. She held senior positions in the National Library of Australia before becoming Deputy Secretary of the Federal Department of Communication and the Arts.

B.A. Santamaria published *Santamaria: A Memoir* in 1997, a revised version of his autobiographical *Against the Tide* (1981).

Patrick Duffield Singleton (1927–)

Patrick Singleton's importance to research at the University of Melbourne is amply demonstrated by the number of theses in which his help is acknowledged. Generations of scholars, from newly enrolled undergraduates daunted by their first encounter with the complexities of a large library, to professors emeritus searching for an elusive reference, benefited from his assistance.

Singleton took his BA in 1948 and MA in Classics the following year. In 1949, he joined the staff of the Australian National University, initially housed in Ormond College. In 1957–58 he worked in the Library of the British Museum of Natural History. This provided experience which was to prove invaluable to students in the University's Botany School, where he conducted an annual bibliographical seminar for advanced students.

From 1959 until his retirement in 1989, Singleton provided reader service to Melbourne staff and students. Many timed their Baillieu visits to coincide with his regular Friday evening shift on desk duty. Although his brief was to assist academic staff and postgraduates, Singleton was frequently to be found taking new library users through the rudiments of searching the catalogue or citing references.

Most of Singleton's working life pre-dated the computer and the access it provides to the holdings of large research libraries, and it is now difficult to recall how much Melbourne scholars relied on one man's acumen in guessing where in the world an elusive book was likely to be found.

With Margaret Murphy, Singleton wrote many case-studies in bibliographical research. He provided biographical information for the History of Australian Science Project. His linguistic expertise, in German, French, Spanish, Italian and Russian, as well as classical Greek and Latin, was in frequent demand.

Singleton was an intrepid traveller and colleagues were entertained both by his accounts of mishaps and adventures in out-of-the way places, and his exceptional mimicry.

❧

Jennifer Anketell Slade (1943–90)

When Jenny Slade joined the City of Springvale in January 1970 as its first Social Worker, she had already worked at Willesmere Hospital, Kew, counselling elderly patients and their families, and had spent four years with the London Borough of Croydon, involved in client counselling and community education and liaison.

Slade graduated BA DipSocStuds from the University of Melbourne in 1966. In 1987, she was awarded an MBA. Her time in England transformed her view of social work and she in turn was to transform the delivery of services to the people of Springvale. She was appointed Manager of Community Services in 1984, a position she occupied until her early death.

At the time of her appointment, welfare services for the municipality consisted of Meals on Wheels, Home Help and Infant Welfare. By 1990, she was responsible for over thirty programs, employing more than seventy full-time staff, and a budget of almost $7 million. She was recognised, in the words of her Chief Executive Officer, as 'the architect of this City's community services'.

Her efforts led to the establishment of the H.L. Williams Court Home for the Frail Aged and she played a crucial role in setting up its management structure and protocols for the assessment of clients. In 1982 an assisted accommodation unit for disabled adults was opened. Slade had alerted Council to the need for this, identified the house in which it could be established and secured its funding. Special housing units for elderly people of non-English-speaking backgrounds were not opened until 1995, but it had been her initiative which secured their funding. Her other achievements included integrating Infant Welfare Services with Community Services, forming the Family Day Care Scheme, developing two child-care centres and establishing Visiting Teacher and Emergency Houses programs.

The sculpture 'Mother and Child' by Ethel Reynolds stands outside the Council Chambers in Springvale as a permanent tribute to her work. The Local Government Community Development and Services Association of Australia administers the Jenny Slade Scholarship established in her memory.

Edward Joseph Sonenberg (1908–89)

E.J. Sonenberg joined the staff of the University in 1922, straight from Carlton State School at the age of fourteen, to work with Alfred Ewart in Baldwin Spencer's Biology School as a junior technical assistant. Current and former staff, speaking of him with admiration and affection, refer to him as 'Sony' but always called him 'Mr Sonenberg' to his face. When he retired in 1973, Sonenberg had been for many years the assistant to the Keeper of the University of Melbourne Herbarium in the School of Botany.

The Herbarium was established in 1926, following the presentation of a considerable collection of predominantly Victorian plant specimens by Herman Montague Rucker Rupp (1872–1956), a clergyman graduate in Natural Science and accomplished botanist. Some of the one hundred thousand specimens currently held in the collection date from the 1850s, and it includes all major plant groups. It is an important aid to the identification of plants in the field.

Sonenberg collected specimens for practical classes so assiduously that long after his retirement students were still using materials he had amassed. Many of these are from the inner suburbs of Melbourne, documenting weeds in particular. He had an exceptional memory and his knowledge of the flora of Victoria, including exotics and poisonous plants, made him well-known and respected throughout the University. His services were frequently called upon by various government authorities such as the Police and by the general public as well as by the Faculties of Agriculture and Veterinary Science.

Sonenberg is remembered by scientists throughout the University for extraordinary diligence—always present at 8.00 a.m. and frequently the last to leave—his kindness to people in distress and his ill-humour on Monday mornings if his beloved Carlton had lost the previous Saturday's football match. A modest and self-effacing man, Sonenberg refused to accept an honorary BSc, on the grounds that he was merely 'blessed with a retentive memory'.

Walter Baldwin Spencer (1860–1929)

The *Australian Dictionary of Biography* tells us that the University's foundation Professor of Biology was 'an approachable, enthusiastic teacher, a brilliant lecturer (in 1902 he packed Melbourne's town hall), a capable and firm administrator, an entrepreneur for national science, one of Victoria's first conservationists (Wilson's Promontory National Park is his monument) and an advocate for Australian artists'.

Baldwin Spencer came from Manchester to take up his appointment in 1887. As well as designing and raising the funds for the biology building, Spencer inaugurated undergraduate field excursions, founded a student science society and inspired the foundation of the Sports Union. He secured the University team's admission to the Victorian Football League in 1908 and was president of the VFL from 1919 to 1926.

Spencer headed the first Australian university department to appoint female academic staff and, when he retired in 1919, all his departmental colleagues were women. He sponsored the Princess Ida club for women and chaired the Professorial Board from 1903 to 1911. He was heavily involved with the National Museum and the National Gallery of Victoria, both of which benefited from his philanthropy as well as from his administrative talents.

It is, however, as an anthropologist and ethnographer that Baldwin Spencer is most remembered. He made several expeditions to central and northern Australia between 1894 and 1926, making representations on Aboriginal welfare to the Australian Parliament in 1913. In 1912 he collected over 200 bark paintings which he presented to the National Museum of Victoria, together with his ethnographic collection, in 1917.

Spencer's interpretation of Aranda society came under criticism at the time and some of his conclusions are paternalistic and unacceptable to later generations. His writings and pictorial records constitute, however, a unique and valuable archive of Aboriginal society.

Spencer had returned to England in 1927, embarking two years later on an anthropological expedition to Tierra del Fuego, where he died on Navarin Island in 1929.

Franz Ferdinand Leopold Stampfl (1913–95)

In 1940, over 2000 German and Austrian men between the ages of eighteen and forty-five, most of whom had fled Nazi persecution, were crammed on board the ship *Dunera* and transported from England to Australia, where they were interned for the rest of the war. Among them were the music critic Felix Werder, the artist Ludwig Hirschfeld-Mack and a Viennese who was to coach some of Australia's greatest runners—Franz Stampfl, who had fled after the Berlin Olympic Games of 1936.

Stampfl had enjoyed a successful coaching career in Northern Ireland before the war, and went back to England in 1946. He worked at Cambridge, Queen's University in Belfast and Oxford University, where he coached Roger Bannister to his record-breaking four-minute mile in 1954. The following year, at the invitation of Melbourne University, he returned to Australia to take up a coaching position in track and field.

In Australia, one of Stampfl's star students was Ron Clarke, the torchbearer for the 1956 Melbourne Olympics, who went on to break seventeen world and twenty-five Australian distance records. Another was Ralph Doubell, who broke a world record when he won the 800 metres race at the 1968 Olympic Games in Mexico City.

Stampfl initiated the technique of 'interval training', which he used to train the three men who broke the four-minute mile under his tutelage: Bannister, Chris Chataway and Christopher Brasher. As well as insisting on scientific precision in his track training, Stampfl put great emphasis on the psychological aspects, commenting that 'every Viennese believes he is another Freud'.

In an extraordinary demonstration of his belief in mind over matter, Stampfl himself continued his coaching career until his death, despite having been made a quadriplegic in a car accident fifteen years earlier.

Stone Family

Emma Constance Stone (1856–1902), her sister Grace Clara Stone (1860–1957) and their cousin Emily Mary Page Stone (1865–1910) changed the medical profession and health care for the poor in Victoria. Their brother, William Stone (1858–1949) was a member of the University's Faculty of Engineering for over thirty years and worked as Chief Electrical Engineer in the newly-formed Electrical Engineering Branch of the Victorian Railways from 1913 to 1920.

First group of female medical students at the University of Melbourne, 1887, Clara Stone seated on the left

Because the University of Melbourne would not admit women to its medical course, Constance Stone took her first degrees in Pennsylvania and London, returning in 1890 to become the first woman to register with the Medical Board of Victoria. Determined to set up a hospital staffed by women for women, she began a part-time practice at Dr Singleton's mission in Collingwood. Her sister Clara Stone was one of the seven women first permitted to enter the Medical School, in 1887. She and Margaret Whyte graduated in 1891, the first two women to do so, and Clara joined her sister's private practice, also working with Dr Singleton.

Mary Stone graduated in 1893 and, despite coming sixth in the final examination, was refused residency at the Melbourne Hospital, which did not admit women residents until 1896. She set up private practice in Windsor, moving later to Hawthorn.

All three women were strongly involved in the professional network of women doctors. The first meeting of the Victorian Medical Women's Society was convened at Constance Stone's house and she was its foundation President. In 1896, eleven doctors resolved to set up their own hospital. What began as an outpatients' dispensary grew, through public subscription, into the Queen Victoria Hospital, opened in 1899.

Constance Stone died of tuberculosis. Her sister continued to practise at the Queen Victoria Hospital until 1919, when she returned entirely to private practice. Mary Stone continued to work at the hospital, as well as being heavily involved with the National Council of Women. An operating theatre in the Queen Victoria Hospital Outpatients' Department was named in her honour.

Frank Strahan (1930–2003)

Frank Strahan was University Archivist at the University of Melbourne from 1960 to 1995. Heading a small unit, for many years independent of and distinct from both the library system and management of University records, Strahan oversaw the creation, management and use of a vital part of the University's research resource.

University Archives has had many addresses since it was set up, moving from various Parkville houses and storage sites to its present position in Brunswick. Many relocations were forced by Strahan's success in attracting deposits of archives, initially from Victorian businesses, and from the mid-1970s, from trade unions, as well as the papers of University staff. Records of all kinds of enterprise are collected. Those of mining companies, such as Western Mining Co., North Broken Hill Ltd and others of the Collins House group, are held as well as the archives of other Australian companies such as Swallow & Ariell Ltd, Foy & Gibson and Hicks Atkinson. In 2004 the Archives began acquiring the Malcolm Fraser Collection—the former Prime Minister's personal papers.

Strahan was for many years associated with the National Trust, chairing its Town Planning and General Advisory Committee from 1970 to 1975 and forming part of its Building Committee from 1961. He was particularly associated with restoration and conservation of Beechworth and with photographs of buildings in Historic Buildings of Victoria. The National Trust honoured his contribution by making him an Honorary Life Member in 1995. In the same year, he was made a Fellow of the Australian Society of Archivists, a high honour as the number of living Fellows is limited to twelve.

Strahan was a longstanding member of the Carlton Association and his interest extended beyond the built environment: for many years, writing as 'Wacker', he contributed the football column to the *Melbourne Times*.

Two of Strahan's children are graduates of the University of Melbourne. Lachlan Strahan (1965–) was appointed Deputy High-Commissioner to India in 2009 and published *Australia's China: Changing Perceptions from the 1930s to the 1990s* (1996) and *Day of Reckoning* (2005).

ℰℐℐ

Sugden Family

On 22 July 1935 the University of Melbourne lost both its Chancellor, Sir John MacFarland, and the first Master of Queen's College, Dr E.H. Sugden.

Edward Holdsworth Sugden (1854–1935) overcame the doubts of some Methodists that a theological institution could co-exist with a university. Queen's College was to become Australia's premier Methodist college and Sugden also achieved the highest church offices, including that of President General of the Methodist Church of Australasia in 1923–26.

During Sugden's forty years as Master, Queen's attracted numerous notable scholars, among them Boyce Gibson, 'Pansy' Wright and Samuel Wadham. His litera-ture tutorials were attended by many non-residents: on two occasions Sugden also took charge of English teaching in the University. He was a bibliophile, and the collection of eighteenth-century editions of the works of John and Charles Wesley which he bequeathed to the College is of international importance.

Sugden was also musical—a friend of A.E. Floyd and supporter, in defiance of Alexander Leeper, of G.W. Marshall-Hall. He was the music critic for the *Argus* and *Australasian* in 1904–12 and played viola in Marshall-Hall's orchestra. The Shakespeare plays performed on the college Foundation Day, in which he directed the students, were renowned. Sugden himself was President of the Melbourne Shakespeare Society in 1914–15. His most important publication, which won him a LittD (1918) from the University, was *A Topographical Dictionary of the Works of Shakespeare and His Fellow Dramatists* (1925). He published other works on literature and music and was the first Chairman of Melbourne University Press as well as a trustee of the Public Library and National Gallery.

Sugden was twice widowed and had six daughters, three from each marriage. One had a distinguished career in the University.

Ruth Sugden (1890–1953) graduated BSc in 1911 and MSc in 1913. From 1921 until her retirement in 1952, she worked in the Chemistry Department. She was responsible for the organisation of junior Chemistry classes, and later for their teaching as well. After dealing for almost twenty years with inadequate and inconvenient facilities, in 1940 she took control of the new facilities, maintaining them so that, in the words of Professor Hartung, they 'drew invariably praise from visitors and warm admiration from her colleagues'. She was also a Council Member and Trustee of Queen's and active both on and off-stage in the Tin Alley Players.

Sydney Sunderland (1910–93)

Sydney Sunderland's undergraduate career at the University of Melbourne, from which he graduated as top student in Medicine in 1935, having come first in every previous year, not only brought him a slew of prizes: it earned him immediate appointment as a Senior Lecturer in Anatomy.

He spent 1937–39 in Oxford and North America, in 1940 taking up the Chair of Anatomy which Melbourne University had offered him in 1938, when he was just twenty-seven years old.

During the war he combined his academic and administrative duties with responsibility for a Peripheral Nerve Injuries Unit at the 115 Australian General Hospital, Heidelberg. The work he did there was to provide a central focus of his research career. Sunderland continued to examine and review 365 patients over a period of ten years after their discharge from hospital. The length of this study, combined with the fact that reparative surgery was undertaken by another surgeon, made it invaluable. Two important books resulted from the work: *Nerves and Nerve Injuries* (1968, 1978) and *Nerve Injuries and Their Repair* (1991).

Sunderland's research won him the honour of presenting the 1979 Founders Lecturer of the American Society for Surgery of the Hand. The establishment of the Sunderland Society, dedicated to the study of peripheral nerve pathology, was an extraordinary tribute to his leadership in the field. At the same time, his teaching was renowned for its care and clarity. He was a Foundation Fellow of the Australian Academy of Science. His governorship of the Ian Potter Foundation from 1964 to 1993 was recognised by the establishment of the annual Sunderland Award. He was Dean of Medicine 1953–71, during which period the number of professors was increased from six to twenty-six, the Brownless Medical Library was built and the Austin Hospital was added to the University's teaching hospitals.

His wife, Nina Gwendoline Sunderland (1918–2003, LLB 1938), graduated in Law from the University of Melbourne. Their son, Ian Sydney Sunderland (1949– , MB BS 1973), is also a Melbourne Medical graduate.

☙

Struan Keith Sutherland (1936–2002)

Government advertisements intended to discourage unauthorised immigration, and travel books such as Bill Bryson's *Down Under*, alike emphasise the prevalence of venomous reptiles and insects in Australia. The life-work of Struan Sutherland was to make these creatures less dangerous.

Sutherland was born in Sydney and educated in Bendigo, graduating in Medicine from the University of Melbourne in 1960. After a short period in the Navy, he began work at the Commonwealth Serum Laboratories in 1966, where he spent almost three decades. During this time he qualified as a specialist physician and pathologist and revolutionised the treatment of poisonous snake and insect bites.

His long search for an antivenom for the venom of the Sydney funnel-web spider ended in 1980 and since that date no-one has died from its bite. He developed a snake venom detection kit which permits doctors to determine which antivenom should be administered to a victim and persuaded medical schools to include the medical management of snake bite in the medical curriculum. Management included the revolutionary pressure-immobilisation technique of first aid, which replaced the use of razor blades and tourniquets.

These discoveries won him international and local recognition, including the Australian Medical Association prize for medical research and the James Cook Medal from the Royal Society of New South Wales. He was a consultant on toxins for the World Health Organization.

When research into antivenom was brought to an end with the privatisation of the CSL in 1994, Sutherland founded the Australian Venom Research Unit in the Department of Pharmacology of Melbourne University.

Sutherland was a prolific author, his books including the autobiographical *A Venomous Life* (1998) and many works for the general public, including *Venomous Creatures of Australia* (1981), *Dangerous Australian Animals and Hydroponics for Everyone* (1986), as well as the standard medical text *Australian Animal Toxins* (1983), most of which have been revised many times. On television, he presented *Holiday Hazards*.

☙

Georgina Sweet (1875–1946)

Science students and staff 1894. Georgina Sweet, front row left

Georgina Sweet (BSc 1896, MSc 1898, DSc 1904) was the foremost parasitologist of her time. She was one of the University's first female science graduates and, in 1904, the first woman to take the degree of Doctor of Science at Melbourne. Her father was an amateur geologist and fellow of the Geological Society, who accompanied Edgeworth David to Funafuti and investigated fossils in the Mansfield district for Frederick McCoy.

On completion of her BSc, Sweet taught at various secondary schools and served on the Association of Secondary Teachers from 1905 to 1912. Despite this, and periods of overseas study during 1913–14 and 1925–27, Sweet's teaching and research career was centred on the University of Melbourne, where she lectured in both the Biology and Veterinary Science schools. In 1915, she was appointed deputy head of the biology school, and from 1916 to 1917, head in Baldwin Spencer's absence. Her students dubbed her, to her amusement, 'Spencer's Faerie Queene'.

Persuaded to apply for the renamed chair in zoology when Spencer retired in 1919, she was passed over in favour of W.E. Agar. She became instead the first Associate Professor of the University. Working in two departments—Zoology and Veterinary Science—took its toll, and Sweet resigned in 1926, continuing to teach for some years as an honorary lecturer.

Despite her punishing workload, Georgina Sweet, a vigorous supporter of women's rights, presided over the council to establish the University Women's College, was an active member and frequently office-bearer of the Lyceum Club, the Young Women's Christian Association, the Victorian Women Graduates' Association and the Pan-Pacific Women's Association, as well as a host of other organisations. She loved travel, undertaking a trek through Africa from the Cape to Cairo with Jessie Webb, and extensive travel in Asia. She was a notable philanthropist and generously supported many University appeals.

&

Jean Tahija (1916–2001)

On the cover of *An Unconventional Woman* (1998), the autobiography of Jean Tahija, is a head and shoulders photograph of a young woman with her fair hair dressed in the fashion of 1942 and a young man in the uniform of the army of the Dutch East Indies. Their marriage, in 1946, was reported in the Melbourne *Herald* under the headline: 'Black Hero Returns for White Wife'. Jean Tahija protested and the adjectives were deleted from later editions. Julius Tahija was a war hero and a nationalist who became a senior government official and held the position of president of Caltex Oil in Indonesia for fifteen years. The couple had two sons and lived in Indonesia after their marriage.

Jean Tahija described her life before marriage as far from conventional. She was the daughter of a policeman whose thinking, in Tahija's words, was ahead of his time: 'Women, he often said to me, should have the same opportunities as men. Every career should be open to them, including the sciences, medicine and dentistry.' When Tahija graduated in Dental Science in 1941, she was only woman in her class of twenty-four. She worked as Registrar at the Dental Hospital for five years before leaving for Indonesia in 1947.

Her husband was equally supportive of her right to a career, commenting that the Moluccas, with a population of over five million, had only one dentist. Practising proved easier said than done. The Dutch dentist at the Macassar hospital refused to employ her, even as a volunteer. Almost four years later, however, an offer to the Jakarta public hospital was accepted. Tahija worked for two years in appalling conditions, grateful for her graduation present from her parents of a set of dental instruments, which she passed to a colleague on her retirement.

Tahija was an enthusiastic horticulturist, establishing a garden at Tugu, which she planted with both native and exotic trees, especially eucalypts and cinnamon. The *Cinnamomum tahijanum* is named for her husband and herself.

☙

William Joseph Thomas (1941–62)

Staff and students returning to the University after the 1962 Easter break were in a state of grief and shock. The 'road carnage' annually bemoaned had claimed a life of national importance. Bill Thomas was twenty-one years old when he died on Easter Sunday and headlines in *Farrago* and the *Bulletin* of 5 May show the impact of his death. The front-page banner of *Farrago* read simply 'Bill Thomas Killed in Crash'. A lengthy eulogy by Vincent Buckley followed. Peter Coleman's obituary in the *Bulletin* was headed 'Death of a Hero'.

Both praise Thomas's political achievements, all the more extraordinary for the fact that, in Buckley's words, 'before he was old enough to possess a vote of his own, he had become one of the men most hated by the coercive forces in the Victorian Labor Party, most liked and admired by the politicians, thinkers and trades union men who opposed those forces'. Coleman noted, 'Bill Thomas was a new type in Australian politics … the student who plays a prominent part in national politics.'

A student of Political Science, Thomas was a frequent contributor to the journals of public affairs. An article excoriating the Victorian ALP Executive's disregard of federal decisions, 'Victoria's Artful Dodgers', was mailed to the *Bulletin* only hours before he died. At the time of his death, he was President of the Melbourne University ALP Club, an organisation which he had revitalised and reformed, turning it into a significant force in Australian political life. He was one of the prime movers of Student Action, a nationwide movement dedicated to the abolition of the White Australia Policy.

If Buckley's prediction that 'the legend that was in full bloom before his death will no doubt continue to grow after it' was not fulfilled, Thomas nonetheless transformed the University for his contemporaries and his death greatly impoverished Australian political life.

☙

William Thwaites (1853–1907)

William Thwaites (BA 1874, MA 1876), who gained his Certificate of Engineering in 1873 and MCE in 1901, is a man to whom inhabitants of what was once called Smellbourne have daily cause to feel grateful.

In 1889, Thwaites gave evidence before the Royal Commission into Melbourne's sanitary conditions and provided a detailed plan for an underground sewerage system. Two years later he was appointed to head the newly formed Melbourne and Metropolitan Board of Works and, modifying the plans put forward by James Mansergh, began one of the city's largest and most enduring construction projects. As well as the obvious public health benefits, the enterprise had the added value of providing direct employment for thousands, and many local contracts, during the Depression. Construction of the sewerage system began in 1892 and the first house connections were made within eight years.

Earlier work by Thwaites also had a lasting effect on Melbourne, notably the Dights Falls scheme to direct fresh water to the lakes of Albert Park and the Botanic Gardens. He was responsible for draining the Port Melbourne lagoon and Elwood swamp as well as swamps in country areas. He designed the Essendon and Caulfield service reservoirs and the Toorourrong reservoir.

Thwaites spent his entire career in Victoria, much of it in Melbourne. He retained his connection with the University as co-examiner in Engineering and a member of Council. He was active in professional organisations as a member of the Victorian Institute of Engineers and Councillor of the Institute of Surveyors. He represented Australasia on the Council of the Institution of Civil Engineers, London, from 1899 to 1901.

William Kent Tickner (1914–2001)

Melbourne Intervarsity Lacrosse team, 1947
William Tickner, centre front row

Bill Tickner (DipCom 1945) was associated with the University of Melbourne from 1932, when he enrolled as a student, until his death in 2001. A University Blue in lacrosse, he joined the administrative staff in 1933 and was appointed as Sub-Registrar of the University's Mildura Branch in 1946. Sports facilities at this campus were far superior to those available to students in Melbourne, with three ovals available for cricket and athletics as well as football.

On his return to Melbourne in 1950, Tickner found a cricket pavilion on sixteen acres of ground and a long narrow field (site of the present Medical school) used for all women's sporting activities and men's running sports. The Beaurepaire Centre, with its extensive coeducational facilities, was established through the generosity of Sir Frank Beaurepaire, largely through the initiative of Bill Tickner and Associate Professor William Rawlinson in the period preceding the 1956 Olympic Games. It was also through their efforts that Sir Frank provided funding for the appointment of Franz Stampfl as Australia's first professional athletics coach.

Bill Tickner was Secretary of the Recreation Grounds Committee and Honorary Secretary of the Melbourne University Sports Union for more than a quarter of a century. Apart from the central achievement of the Beaurepaire Centre, this period saw the creation of the running track, of new tennis courts and the main oval as well as the upgrading of the boat sheds and the acquisition of the ski-lodge and shooting and mountaineering facilities.

Tickner was a significant figure in inter-university competitions, being at various times the University's delegate to the Australian Universities Sports Association and Australian delegate to the Federation of International University Sport. During his time at the University the number of sporting clubs almost doubled, from twenty-five to forty-two. Bill Tickner was made a Member of the Order of Australia in 1989.

✌

Tipping Family

James Tipping (1852–1912) was the only one of his parents' seven children to survive infancy. In contrast, five of his six children reached the age of eighty and his youngest child, Minnie, died in 1995 at the age of 104.

Martha, James and Minnie Tipping, 1911

Although not all the Tippings were teachers, the history of the family is intimately entwined with that of education in Victoria, both Catholic and State. Members taught over a period of forty-three years in ten Victorian state schools, including Bendoc, Bonegilla, Stanley and Monbulk. James's children attended his classes before completing their education at private schools.

Martha Bergin Tipping (1883–1966), was an early woman graduate from Melbourne University, taking her BA in 1903 and MA the following year. Having completed her course under Victorian Education Department sponsorship, she was posted to various country and metropolitan schools, including Melbourne High and the University Practising School (later University High). She taught until 1915, when she resigned, as women were obliged to do, upon marrying. One of her sons, Edmund Muirhead (1927–), is a Principal Fellow in the School of Physics. Martha Tipping continued teaching after her marriage, coaching trainee nuns and priests as well as senior pupils from St Kevin's College in French.

Elinora Mary Ursula Tipping (1891–1995), known as Minnie, interrupted her university studies to take the veil, entering the Loreto Convent in Ballarat in 1912. On being received into the Order in 1914, she took the name of Mother Mary Francis Borgia. She returned to the University and took her degree in 1928. Mother Borgia made a significant contribution to the development of Catholic education and was remarkable for her involvement with the outside world, even at a period when the Loreto community existed as a semi-enclosed religious order.

Martha and Minnie Tipping's nephew, E.W. (Bill) Tipping (1916–70), will be remembered by older readers as the author of the 'In Black and White' column in the Melbourne *Herald* and his work for improving provision of care to mentally disabled children. He appeared regularly on television on *Meet the Press* and won a Walkley Award in 1960 for his reporting of the Sharpeville Massacre in South Africa.

Samuel John Tong-Way (1894–1988)

Visitors to the Gryphon Gallery in the 1888 Building may note a name on the Honour Roll of students from the Melbourne Teachers' College who returned from World War I which stands out from those around it. Samuel John Tong-Way is the sole Australian of Chinese descent.

He was no newcomer to this country. His father had followed his own father to the goldfields around 1885. The Reverend J. Tong-Way was ordained in the Presbyterian ministry in Ballarat in 1905.

Before entering the Teachers' College in 1914, Tong-Way worked as a probationer in Dean School in the Maryborough District and Humffray Street School in Ballarat. He tried to enlist in 1916 but was rejected on medical grounds. In 1917 he graduated with a Graduate Diploma in Education. In June of the same year he was accepted for military service. He embarked in May 1918 and was sent from the Divisional Signallers in Egypt to France in September 1918. His brother, Hedley, also enlisted.

In February 1919, rather than returning directly to Australia, Tong-Way chose to go to London, undertaking courses in science at London University, History and Latin at Oxford and Pedagogy at the London Day Training College. He returned to Australia in February 1920 and graduated BA in 1921.

By March 1920 he was embarked on a career with the Victorian Education Departments which was to continue until his retirement in 1960. Once retired, he taught Leaving Certificate History at Girton College, Bendigo.

Tong-Way's examiners reported on him as 'Zealous, progressive and thorough; has shown excellent organizing ability both in directing the activities of his school and as district Gould League organizer; is held in high esteem by the community.' He expressed it differently, telling Morag Loh, 'I had fought for the country and therefore I should work for the country as well.' He was active in the Freemasons and RSL and Senior Citizens, as well as bowling and golfing.

Tong-Way lived to the age of ninety-three and is buried in the cemetery at Kangaroo Flat. His daughter Margery (1932–) graduated from the Teachers' College and won scholarships to the Courtauld Institute and Harvard.

His son David (1943–) is a landscape ecologist who worked for almost forty years with CSIRO and in countries as varied as Iran, Spain, the USA and Iceland. He was awarded the prize for excellence by the Australian Minerals and Energy Environmental Foundation for his contribution to mine-closure methodology in 2000.

☙❧

William George Dismore Upjohn (1888–1979)

William Upjohn's association with the University of Melbourne began in 1906, when he enrolled in Medicine. He retired as its Chancellor in 1967. He did not retire from surgery at the same time, however, but continued to practise until 1977.

Graduating MB in 1909, Upjohn began a connection which lasted seventy years, being appointed Resident Medical Officer at the Royal Melbourne Hospital in 1910. After graduating MD (1912) and MS (1913), he served with distinction in World War I as a specialist surgeon in France, for which he was mentioned in despatches.

Upjohn was especially noted for his skill in grafting. He was a Fellow of the Royal College of Surgeons of England and Foundation Fellow of the Royal Australian College of Surgeons. A Fellow of the Australian Medical Association, Upjohn was also a member of the Victorian Council of the British Medical Association and its Honorary Librarian, as well as President of the Victorian Branch in 1933–34. He also lectured at the University in Anatomy and Surgery.

As well as occupying various surgical positions in the Royal Melbourne Hospital, Upjohn was its President in 1960–68. He also served on the Hospital and Charities Commission and the Victorian Medical Benevolent Society. After a period as Deputy Chancellor of the University (1962–66), he became Chancellor in 1966–67.

A comment by Upjohn in the centenary edition of the *Royal Melbourne Hospital Clinical Reports* (1948) gives an indication of the changes through which he lived. 'Formerly, if you saw a man with a badly gashed shin and compound fracture of both leg bones, you might be right if you guessed he had been kicked by a horse, but if you saw the same injury now in a young man you would almost certainly be right if you guessed it was a motor cycle injury.'

The Sir William Upjohn Medal is awarded every five years for distinguished services to medicine in Australia.

Jessie Mary Vasey (1897–1966)

Jessie Halbert was born in Roma, Queensland. She was educated at Lauriston Girls' School and Methodist Ladies' College. She married George Vasey in 1921, the year she graduated BA from the University of Melbourne.

George Alan Vasey (1895–1945) was a career soldier who had served with the AIF at Gallipoli and on the Western Front. Jessie Vasey accompanied her husband to Quetta after the World War I. At the outbreak of World War II, he was posted to Libya and commanded the Australian forces in Crete. From 1942 until his death in a plane crash in Far North Queensland, he served in several key campaigns in New Guinea.

While her husband served in Europe, Vasey worked with the AIF Women's Association and established the War Widows' Craft Guild, which supported Legacy and the RSL, and established accommodation of its own for war widows. In 1951 it set up eight bed-sitting rooms—by 1963, it had created housing worth £1 million.

Widowed in 1945 with two children, Vasey founded the War Widows' Guild, recruiting members from the 10,000 Australian women widowed by World War II. She was a formidable campaigner for the welfare of war widows and their children, visiting each state of Australia. As well as raising money for housing, Vasey lobbied successfully for improvements in pensions and health benefits.

Her advocacy for recognition and financial support was uncompromising:

Australia's wealth and future were paid for in blood and sweat and tears … The war widow has paid the greatest price … If a man gave his life the nation called him a hero. But it gave his widow a shoddy badge and ruined her and her family financially … I do not regard it as a pension—but as the country's debt to the men who died in its defence.

Vasey died in a car crash in 1966. She is commemorated in a number of awards in Australian universities, including the Jessie Vasey Prize in Women's History at her Alma Mater.

Mechai Viravaidya (1941–)

In Thailand, a condom is popularly known as a 'Mechai' in tribute to the work of Mechai Viravaidya, chairman and founder of the Population and Community Development Association. Founded in 1974, the nonprofit PDA is active in the field of family planning, rural development and HIV/AIDS prevention.

Khun Mechai was educated at Geelong Grammar and graduated in Commerce in 1964. He was awarded an honorary Doctorate of Laws from the University of Melbourne in 1993. He holds many other honorary degrees and decorations from the Thai and Australian governments for his work in population control and poverty reduction. His biography, *From Condoms to Cabbages*, by Thomas D'Agnes, was published in 2001.

The title refers to a chain of restaurants established to promote the aims of the PDA. The 'world's largest collection of national brand condoms' adorns the walls and condoms are offered in place of the more usual after-dinner mints. A handicraft shop associated with the Bangkok restaurant, jointly operated by PDA and Oxfam, sells condom-related artefacts as well as more traditional craft work from Northeast Thailand.

Khun Mechai is a frequent speaker at international forums on the necessity for increasing efficiency and entrepreneurial activity among non-government organisations as they evolve to fill the role previously taken by governments in the alleviation of poverty and elimination of disease. He believes donors will increasingly direct their assistance towards world crises and that non-government organisations must therefore be prepared to use business enterprises to finance their ongoing programs.

He is also outspoken on the issue of international assistance in dealing with the challenge presented by the spread of HIV/AIDS, arguing that local political and financial commitment are of the first importance, and noting that 96 per cent of the money spent in Thailand on HIV/AIDS prevention was raised locally. He is also a Senator who has occupied several government posts. His awards include the Bill and Melinda Gates Award for Global Health in 2007.

Samuel McMahon Wadham (1891–1972)

Samuel Wadham, left

Samuel Wadham, who came to Melbourne from Cambridge in 1926 as Professor of Agriculture and became Dean of the Faculty the following year, was only the second occupant of the Chair. From 1905 until that time the Faculty had had a succession of Deans, staff substantively employed in other Departments and low student numbers. Wadham was to remain Dean for thirty years.

Geoffrey Blainey has described the situation which greeted Wadham. The University Council was at first reluctant to appoint a person it believed to be a 'laboratory man' rather than someone who would 'get amongst the farming community'. Their fears were groundless, as Council discovered when Wadham, asked to accept a five-year contract rather than a tenured position, prepared to return to Cambridge in 1931. The outcry from agricultural organisations across the state made clear the extent to which the rural community had come to admire and respect him.

Wadham believed that agricultural science could only be taught successfully in combination with a solid grounding in general science and the economic context within which agriculture operates. During his time at the University, some four hundred students graduated in Agricultural Science.

Wadham's commitment to outreach was exemplified in his membership of many government bodies, ranging from the Commonwealth Dairy Committee, the Royal Commission on Wheat Bread and Flour Industries and the Rural Reconstruction Commission to the Immigration and Planning Council from 1949 to 1959. He served on the Martin Committee on Tertiary Education in Australia, the Council of CSIRO and as President of both the Royal Society of Victoria and ANZAAS.

He also made hundreds of radio broadcasts, speaking on all aspects of rural life. He became one of the University's best-known public figures. His published works include *Australian Farming, 1788–1965* (1967), *The Land and the Nation* (1943) and *Land Utilization in Australia* (1939). A biography, *Wadham: Scientist for Land and People* by L.R. Humphreys, was published in 2000.

ల

Jessie Stobo Watson Webb (1880–1944)

Orphaned at the age of nine, Jessie Webb developed into a strong and independent woman, graduating with first class honours in history and political economy and in logic and philosophy (BA 1902, MA 1904) She was appointed to the History Department in December 1908, teaching British history as well as her special subject, Ancient History, and left it only on her death. She was Acting Professor during her last illness and continued to administer the Department from her hospital bed. She was appointed senior lecturer in 1923, and Acting Professor in 1925, in 1933–34 and again in 1942–44.

In 1922 and 1923 she toured Africa with Georgina Sweet, followed by eight months at the British School of Archaeology at Athens, when she travelled extensively in Greece, notably to the excavations at Mycenae and Knossos. Webb's belief in the importance of such fieldwork was exemplified in her bequest to the University to form a fund 'to send every five years a student to spend a season in Greece'. Also in 1923, Webb was an alternate delegate to the League of Nations Assembly.

Webb was involved in many women's initiatives. She was a founder of University Women's College, of the Victorian Women Graduates' Association, of which she was President 1924–25, and of the Lyceum Club, over which she presided from 1920 to 1922.

In 1926, Jessie Webb travelled with a fellow member of the Lyceum Club, Alice Anderson, to Central Australia. Anderson was the proprietor of a garage, chauffeur service and driving school in Kew, which employed only women mechanics and drivers. The pair travelled in a Baby Austin car, accomplishing the difficult journey to Alice Springs and back in six weeks.

Jessie Webb served under three Professors of History: Elkington, Scott and Crawford. She was instrumental in the appointment of Kathleen Fitzpatrick and her contribution to historical scholarship is permanently commemorated in the Jessie Webb Scholarship, which she endowed.

Ivy Lavinia Weber (1892–1976)

Ivy Weber was left a widow for the second time in 1930 when her husband, the athlete and educationist Clarence Weber, died, leaving her with eleven children. She believed girls should put 'marriage and motherhood before any other career', but by dint of 'working a tremendous amount of overtime', she led a successful public life.

Weber became the first woman to win a seat in a general election in the Victorian Parliament. She won and held the seat of Nunawading in three successive contests between 1937 and 1943, as one of three candidates endorsed by the newly formed League of Women Electors of Victoria, of which she was the president. An independent, she generally supported the Country Party government. Her electoral platform included a true democracy to provide economic security, free education from kindergarten to University, a National Health Scheme, slum eradication and housing for the poor, and a comprehensive national insurance scheme which would cover hospital treatment. In parliament she lobbied for female representation on government boards, equal pay for teachers, women's right to serve on juries and a homemaker's allowance for women with families.

Before entering parliament, Weber lectured on figure control at the Berlei Corset Company, gave radio talks on physical culture and served on bodies as varied as the Playgrounds Association, the Red Cross, the Australian Temperance Council, the Women's Christian Temperance Union and the National Fitness Council. As an executive member of the National Council of Women, she played a leading part in the establishment of the physical education course at the University of Melbourne, which was the first in Australia.

Weber resigned her state seat in 1943 and unsuccessfully contested the Federal seat of Henty as part of the League of Women Voters' Women for Canberra Movement. She was also unsuccessful in contesting the state seat of Box Hill in 1945. She subsequently held administrative positions with the Department of Supply, the Country Party and the Women's Movement Against Socialism.

☙❧

Leonard William Weickhardt (1908–2000)

Len Weickhardt had a highly distinguished career in industry and education as well as in the University of Melbourne. During his time with ICI Australia he was, with J.R.A. Glenn and David Zeidler, responsible for creating a research department within the company. During World War II a team led by Weickhardt, Glenn and F. Lament established a plant to produce the antimalarial drug sulphamerazine. Although this proved no more effective than atebrin, which was already in use by the troops in New Guinea, it was an important step in the creation of paludrine.

Weickhardt was born in Ballarat and educated at various state schools and the Working Men's College (which is now the RMIT University) before taking his MSc from Melbourne University in 1928. From 1935 to 1938 he worked at ICI in England, where he also met and married his wife of fifty-two years, Florence Blenkharn, a teacher. They returned to Australia and Weickhardt rose to become Executive and Research Director of ICI Australia, a position he occupied from 1955 to 1972. John Poynter has noted that this period was exceptionally fruitful in terms of cooperation between University scientists, CSIRO and business, with ICI proving especially helpful to the Faculty of Agriculture.

When Weickhardt succeeded Sir Robert Menzies as Chancellor in 1972 he had been a member of the University Council for a decade, proving especially adept in dealing with the student unrest and financial difficulties of the 1960s. His interest in education extended beyond the University: he chaired the National Council of Independent Schools and was General President of the Royal Australian Chemical Institute, and chaired the Boards of the Royal Melbourne Hospital and Victorian Committee of the Ludwig Institute for Cancer Research. His *Masson of Melbourne* (1989) won the Olle Prize.

Len and Florence Weickhardt's son, Philip Weickhardt (1948– , BSc 1970, MSc 1972) was Managing Director and Chief Executive Officer of Orica, formerly ICI Australia Ltd, 1997–2001. He was appointed as a Commissioner with the Productivity Commission in 2004 and was Chairman of Earthwatch Institute 2002–11.

Harold Leslie White (1905–92)

Sir Harold White is Australian librarianship's only recipient of a knighthood. Born in Numurkah, he graduated in Arts from the University of Melbourne after attending Wesley College. In 1923 he joined the staff of the Commonwealth Parliamentary Library in Melbourne, moving to Canberra with the federal parliament in 1927. Until 1967 the Commonwealth Parliamentary Librarian was also National Librarian, and White held the combined position until 1968, when he oversaw the separation of the Parliamentary and National libraries.

Under his direction the National Library of Australia became one of the premier research institutions of the country, with collections extending far beyond Australiana, and an outreach service which encompassed running public library services in the Northern Territory and the ACT, as well as stocking the libraries of Australia's diplomatic posts. White's determination in pursuing private collections in Europe and the United Kingdom was legendary, matched only by his skill at securing funding for their acquisition from successive Prime Ministers. As well as the great Australiana collections of Ferguson, Nan Kivell and Matthews, the resources acquired were as varied as the David Nichol Smith Collection of eighteenth-century literature, the Kashnor Collection on the political economy of Britain and Ireland, the Gayer-Anderson Collection of Indian paintings and drawings from the seventeenth to nineteenth centuries, the Braga Collection on the Portuguese in Asia and the Yves Coffin collection of 1000 photographic prints of Javanese architecture.

The long-awaited move into the new building on the shores of Lake Burley Griffin in 1968 was described by White as the promised land after forty years in the wilderness. He had taken a personal interest in every aspect of its development.

White chaired the advisory committee on *The Australian Encyclopedia* and the Advisory Council on Bibliographical Services. He is remembered in the Harold White Fellowships awarded annually for research conducted using the resources he did so much to build. Sir Harold was the father of David White (1931–2004), pro-Vice-Chancellor 1975–78 and Professor of Microbiology 1967–94.

☙❧

Williams Family

All six children of William and Helen Williams were educated at Melbourne University. Although money was tight in this clergyman's household, there was always enough to buy books. The four sons were all residents of Queen's College.

W. Kenneth Williams (1915–40) was set for a brilliant career in Economics when he enlisted, hoping to protect his younger brothers from the call-up. He was shot down over the North Sea in Bomber Command. Bruce Williams (1919–2010) took his Economics degree, winning the Wyelaskie Scholarship as Ken had done before him. In 1940 he went to Adelaide University and found himself

Back row, from left: *Bruce, Colin, Gwen, Morris* Front row, from left: *Ken, Helen, William and Ruth*

in charge of the Department of Economics. His career, after appointments at Belfast, Keele and Manchester, culminated in his appointment from 1967 to 1981 as Vice-Chancellor and Principal of Sydney University. He chaired the Committee of Inquiry into Education and Training, 1976–79.

Morris Williams (1920–2001) spent nineteen years in the Faculty of Education at the University after teaching at Wesley College. He was a notable cricketer with a second career as a baritone. Runner-up in the 1946 Sun Aria competition, he performed with the Melbourne Symphony Orchestra under such notable conductors as Goossens and Barbirolli.

Colin Williams (1921–99) studied History and Theology and was Professor of Systematic Theology at Queen's College. As Dean of the Yale University Divinity School from 1969 to 1979, he appointed women to the Faculty and created the first full-time positions for Catholics. He is reported to have once raised an urgently needed six million dollars in a single morning, making only six telephone calls!

Ruth Williams (1926–2001) graduated in Music, majoring in piano and viola. She taught piano at MLC for many years. Gwenyth Williams (1917–2011) did not complete her Commerce degree because, inspired by her brother's death, she took up nursing. She had a distinguished career as the first Nurse Executive Officer of the Hospital and Charities Commission, notably setting up bursaries similar to those offered to trainee teachers. In 1956, as secretary to John La Nauze in the History Department, she began her second career, succeeding Ray Erickson as departmental manager and appointed Organising Tutor, with responsibility for organising courses for the Honours students. Gwen's career in the University extended well beyond normal, as successive Sub-Deans of Arts brought her out of retirement to assist in student selection.

Worner Brothers

Howard (left) and Hill Warner (right)

Both Howard Knox Worner (1913–2006) and his brother Hill Wesley Worner (1917–2002) chaired the Department of Metallurgy at Melbourne University and were Deans of the Faculty, although the elder spent more of his working life in the mining industry.

Howard Worner (BSc 1934, MSc 1936, DSc 1942) was born in Swan Hill and came to the University from the Bendigo School of Mines. After a year as Demonstrator in Metallography, he was appointed Lecturer in 1936. In 1939–46 he was Research Fellow at the Dental Materials Research Laboratory, returning to the University as Professor of Metallurgy, which position he occupied until 1946.

In 1956 he left to become Director of Research at Broken Hill Pty Ltd. As Director, New Process Development at CRA Ltd in 1964–75 he developed the WORCRA continuous smelting and refining process. After 1975, Worner held a variety of industry positions, including a period as Chairman, Victorian Brown Coal Council and Director of the Microwave and Materials Research Institute at the University of Wollongong. He was awarded an Honorary DEng in 1983 and the Benjamin F. Fairless Award in 2002.

Hill Wesley Worner (BSc 1936, MSc 1938, DSc 1953) assumed the Chair of Metallurgy ten years after his brother had left it. He returned to the University after a career which had included work with CSIR and the Canadian Mines Board. He was Professor of Metallurgy 1956–75, leaving to take up the position of Director of the Institute for Industrial Technology of CSIRO in 1979.

When a 135–metre section of the Westgate Bridge collapsed during construction in 1970, Hill Worner was one of the consultants immediately called in to investigate. Thirty-five people were killed in this accident, with a further eighteen injured.

Howard and Hill Worner are not the only brothers to have both occupied Chairs in the Engineering Faculty. Earlier, William Charles Kernot, the foundation professor appointed in 1882, had been followed, though not immediately on his retirement, by his brother Wilfred Noyce Kernot, Professor of Engineering from 1932 to 1936.

෴

Roy Douglas Wright (1907–1990)

'Pansy' Wright shares with Anthony Brownless the distinction of having been a Professor at the University before his appointment as Chancellor. He never lost daily, informal contact with his colleagues in all areas and could be seen, until shortly before his death, queuing up for lunch at University House and joining a convivial table, seemingly at random.

Wright studied briefly at the University of Tasmania before transferring to Melbourne to study Medicine in 1925. Apart from a period in 1937–39 working with Howard Florey in England, he was to remain here until his death. This institutional loyalty resulted from no parochial outlook: returning from Oxford convinced him that Australian institutions were under-resourced

Left to right: *Victor Trikojus, Howard Florey and R.D. Wright*

and under-valued, and Wright set about changing the face of Australian scientific and medical research.

His career included appointments as Professor of Physiology, 1939–71; Medical Director of the Peter MacCallum Institute, 1971–75; Deputy Chancellor, 1972–80; and Chancellor, 1980–89.

Florey praised the young Wright's 'real flair for experimental work'. The variety of topics which engaged his interest is indeed astonishing, ranging from work on the blood supply to the liver and lung, his early, groundbreaking enunciation of the evolutionary benefit of the folding of the cerebral cortex, and, during the War, the development of a lightweight, fire-resistant flying suit for pilots.

With his younger colleagues Derek Denton and Victor Wynn, Wright founded the Ionic Research Unit in 1948, the forerunner of the Howard Florey Institute. Wright played a central role as leader of a brilliant research team in the department of Physiology. It is, however, as a scientific administrator and civil libertarian that Wright is best remembered. He was instrumental in the establishment of the Peter MacCallum Cancer Institute, the Australian National University, including the John Curtin School of Medical Research, the new Medical School at the University, as well as the Florey.

Wright never shied from controversy. His ten-year battle after 1956 on behalf of Sidney Sparkes Orr, who had been dismissed by the University of Tasmania, found him defending a difficult man, but he was unwavering in his defence of academic freedom.

'Pansy' anecdotes abound in University history. Many are apocryphal: most of them are not. '*Pansy': A Life of Roy Douglas Wright* by Peter McPhee was published in 1999.

Picture credits

Unless otherwise stated, images are taken from the University of Melbourne Archives

à Beckett	Private collection, courtesy of Naughton's Hotel
Allan	CSIRO Archives
Austral	National Library of Australia
Bage	Women's College, University of Queensland
Ball	University of Melbourne History Department
Blackburn	Parliament of Victoria
Blainey	National Library of Australia
Bourke Family	Monash University
Bourke, Margaret	Portrait by Donald Cameron in Kilbreda College
Bourke, Merilyn	Private collection
Brookes	Royal Women's Hospital
Brown Family	University of Melbourne Faculty of Engineering
Browne	Portrait by Nornie Gude in Don Garden, *The Melbourne Teacher Training Colleges*
Buckley	Portrait by Alec Bolton in National Library of Australia
Burhop	*Biographical Memoirs of Fellows of the Royal Society 1981*
Button	Photo by Jennifer Herold, courtesy Text Publishing
Cade	American Psychiatric Association
Callil	Private collection
Campbell	National Archives of Australia
Challen	Ted Roche Studio
Chamberlin	*UniNews*
Cherry	University of Melbourne Medical History Museum
Clarke	Janet Clarke Hall
Coppel	Private collection
Cordner	Private collection
Cran	*Farrago*
Crespin	Geological Society of Australia
Cussen	Leo Cussen Institute
Dara	Victorian Women's Trust
Deakin	National Library of Australia
Davies	Private collection
Ducker	Private collection
Falk Family	From *The Half-open Door*, Hale & Iremonger, 1982
Fenner	University of Ballarat
Fitzpatrick	Photograph by Helmut Newton
Gawler	Private collection
Gizycki	Private collection

Grishin	Private collection
Harding	Private collection
Henderson	University of Melbourne Faculty of Economics and Commerce
Hibberd	Hume Dow, *Memories of Melbourne University* (Hutchinson)
Hii	Pier Carthew
Hoadley	Private collection
Horacek	Private collection
Inagaki	National Archives of Australia: B13; 1926/13464
Isaacs	National Library of Australia
Jackson	Private collection
Karagheusian	University House, University of Melbourne
Knopfelmacher	University of Melbourne Psychology Department
Lloyd-Green	Private collection
MacCallum	University of Melbourne Medical History Museum
McCloskey	Private collection
Macknight	Private collection
Macnamara	National Portrait Gallery, courtesy Merran Samuel
Marginson	Private collection
Millis, Jean	Private collection
Moshinsky	Private collection
Mushin	*Australian Jewish News*
Palmer	National Library of Australia
Pietzcker	Courtesy Michael Meszaros
Preston	University of Melbourne Medical History Museum
Rubbo	*Chiron*, 2010, University of Melbourne Faculty of Medicine
Saffin	Private collection
Samuel	*University Gazette*
Singleton	Private collection
Slade	Private collection
Sonenberg	Private collection
Stampfl	Private collection
Sugden	Private collection
Tahija	Penguin Books
Thomas	*Farrago*
Thwaites	Board of Works
Tipping	John Tipping, *Bush Teachers of Victoria*
Tong Way	Private collection
Wadham	University Gazette
Weber	Portrait by Nancy Moffatt, Victorian Parliament
White	National Library of Australia
Williams Family	Private collection

Subject Index

(Note: Many names will appear in more than one category)

Maxwell

Samuel

Law

Blackburn

Brennan

Coppel

Cowen

Cussen

Deakin

Evans

Fink

Ford

Foster

Gavan Duffy

Hearn

Higgins

Isaacs

Marginson

Menzies

Moshinsky

Santamaria

Libraries and Archives

Barry

Lodewycks

Matthaei

Singleton

Strahan

Literature and Publishing

Bourke

Buckley

Callil

Christesen

Fink

Garner

Grattan

Humphries

Medley

Murray-Smith

Palmer

Rubbo

Medicine and Allied Sciences

a'Beckett

Agar

Allan

Amies

Bage

Barrett

Bourke

Brown

Brownless

Bryce

Burnet

Cade

Campbell

Cherry

Cleary

Coates

Cookson

Cordner

De Garis

Ducker

Dyason

Fenner

Gizycki

Gröbner

Hibberd

Jackson

Leeper

Lloyd-Green

MacCallum

McCloskey

Macknight

McLennan

Macnamara

Marginson

Matthaei

Millis

Mushin

Pietzcker

Preston

Rubbo

Sonenberg

Stone

Sunderland

Sutherland

Sweet

Tahija

Upjohn

Wadham

Wright

Performing Arts

Andrews

Austral

Brookes

Dara

Garner

Grainger

Harding

Heinze

Hibberd

Hii

Humphries

Jones

Lloyd-Greene

McCaughey

Marshall-Hall

Moshinsky

Murray-Smith

Rubbo

Williams

Philosophy and Psychology
Davies
Falk
Gibson

Physical Sciences
Boas
Brown
Burhop
Cran
Crespin
Falk
Hoadley
Kernot
Laby
Law
Leeper
McCoy
MacFarland
Masson
Matthaei
Monash
Moorhouse
Nanson
Sugden
Thwaites
Weickhardt
Worner

Politics and Public Policy
Ball
Blackburn
Button
Cairns
Challen
Dara
Davies
Deakin
Evans

Fink
Gavan Duffy
Hamer
Hearn
Knopfelmacher
McCaughey
Marginson
Menzies
Nanson
Palmer
Santamaria
Slade
Thomas
Vasey
Weber

Sport
a'Beckett
Bage
Clark
Cordner
Cowen
Cropley
Cussen
Dyason
Foster
Gorman
Hamer
Higgins
Landy
Law
MacCallum
Macknight
Spencer
Stampfl
Tickner
Tong-Way

Statistics
Allan

University Administration
a'Beckett
Amies
Barrett
Barry
Brownless
Clarke
Elliott
Marcham
Marginson
Medley
Menzies
Nanson
Polglaze
Priestley
Weickhardt
Williams
Wright

University House
Karagheusian
Moorhouse
Marginson
Matthaei

Veterinary Science
Andrews
Chamberlin
Gawler
Mushin
Sweet

Visual Arts
Harding
Hii
Horacek
Humphries
McCaughey